The Ar
FINE WOODTURNING

Projects &
Inspiration for
Every Turner

S. Gary Roberts

STERLING

New York / London
www.sterlingpublishing.com

DEDICATION

This book would not have been possible without the encouragement and constant loving support of
my life partner, best friend, and loving wife, Imagene "Gene" Conro Roberts.
We dedicate this effort to the future generations of woodturners and ask that they
ENJOY TURNING!

Designed by Judy Morgan

Library of Congress Cataloging-in-Publication Data

Roberts, S. Gary.
    Masterful woodturning : projects & inspiration for the skilled
turner / S. Gary Roberts.
          p. cm.
    Includes index.
    ISBN 0-8069-8709-X
    1. Turning I. Title.
TT203 .R63 2000
684'.083–dc21   00-037290

10 9 8 7 6 5 4 3 2 1

Published by Sterling Publishing Company, Inc.
387 Park Avenue South, New York, N.Y. 10016
© 2000 by S. Gary Roberts
Previously published under the title *Masterful Woodturning: Projects &
Inspiration for the Skilled.*
Distributed in Canada by Sterling Publishing
c/o Canadian Manda Group, 165 Dufferin Street
Toronto, Ontario, Canada M6K 3H6
Distributed in the United Kingdom by GMC Distribution Services
Castle Place, 166 High Street, Lewes, East Sussex, England BN7 1XU
Distributed in Australia by Capricorn Link (Australia) Pty. Ltd.
P.O. Box 704, Windsor, NSW 2756, Australia

Sterling ISBN-13: 978-1-4027-5720-4
     ISBN-10: 1-4027-5720-4

For information about custom editions, special sales, premium and
corporate purchases, please contact Sterling Special Sales
Department at 800-805-5489 or specialsales@sterlingpublishing.com.

Special appreciation to Better Homes & Garden's
Wood magazine editor for permission to use three
of my previously published projects as a portion of
this presentation, including Project No. 20 from the
January 1995 issue.

Also thanks to *Amercian Woodturner* journal for allowing me to adapt five of my previously published
projects: Nos. 1 and 2 from December 1993; No. 7
from December 1996; No. 22; and No. 29 from
March 1996.

CONTENTS

Introduction   6

Lathe Safety Guidelines, Sanding Suggestions, Finishes, Lathe Indexing

1. Mesquite Vessel   12
2. Viny Mesquite Decanter   18
3. By the Numbers   23
4. Mesquite Twister   28
5. Shell-Carved Vertical Hollow Flask   33
6. Another Blooming Mesquite   37
7. Turned Wine-Bottle Stand   42
8. Twig-Pot Fun   46
9. Scrap-Wood Music Box   49
10. Music Box Ballet   52
11. Bird-Watchers' Carousel Music Box   55
12. Flying-Saucer Music Box   59
13. Lidded Box with Push-Button Music Box   66
14. Traditional Turned Music Box   69
15. "Let the Good Times Roll" Music Box   72
16. Horses Carousel Music Box   77
17. Flying Birds Carousel Music Box   80
18. Thread Dispenser with Hidden Drawer   84
19. Sewing Tidy with Thimble   89
20. Spool Tidy   93
21. Pinwheel-Swirl Vessel   101
22. Rings of Saturn   105
23. Scallop-Shell Lidded Box   109
24. Scales of Justice   113
25. Carved-Edge Platter   118
26. Candleholder with Carved-through Chimney   121
27. Hollow Flask   124
28. Handled Urn   128
29. Mashrabeya Vessel   132
30. Carved-through Lidded Vessel   138
31. Spiral-Grooved Vessel   144
32. Floral Carved Vessel   147
33. Izzy A. Turner   151

Index   159

Metric Equivalents   160

ACKNOWLEDGMENTS—

❖ Imagene "Gene" Conro Roberts

First and foremost, my wife, "Gene," who has been steadfast in her encouragement and support of my fascination with woodworking. She has done everything from giving design suggestions to being the judge and critic of the end product. In addition, she has spent endless hours of unselfish time at the computer to word process and make legible my excuse for longhand and the Texas language.

❖ Brenda Roberts Ermis

Brenda, our daughter, has smiled and enthusiastically encouraged our effort by correcting our computer errors. Only those who have a loving relationship with a daughter can understand that special sense of pride that is accompanied by this honor. Thank you, Babe!

❖ Larry Del Roberts

No effort I have ever made in woodturning has been without a thought of gratitude to my brother, Larry Del Roberts, who not only gave me my first lesson on a lathe, but has helped me with equipment and encouragement. He has always been the true embodiment of "Brotherly Love."

❖ American Association of Woodturners

When we were helping found and nurture the American Association of Woodturners, no one ever thought that it would become the vehicle to carry all turners to higher levels than we would have ever dreamed. To this fine association we all must pay our debt of gratitude by openly sharing with others as they have shared with us. The Association's many proud achievements would not have happened without the unselfish dedication, personal sacrifices, and hard work of the volunteer turners who have served as officers, directors, and advisors. We deeply thank you.

My Special Thanks for the Following

❖ Illustrations

Barry L. Bennett, of Austin, Texas, is an engineer and specialist in converting project plans to computer-generated drawings. Barry is a fellow turner and carver. He has used unbounded patience to convert my rough sketches and drawings into works of computer art.

❖ Photography

Terry Mueller, of Austin, Texas, is a professional photographer and has been a great asset to the visual depictions of the works that are included in this book.

❖ Proofreading

Stacy Hager, of Austin, Texas, is a friend and fellow woodturner. His educational background and experience in authoring papers for the University of Texas have been invaluable in this monumental effort. His translation of my Texas language to understandable directions in English has been deeply appreciated. You can see that he, too, enjoys turning.

THIS MAJESTIC TREE

What ancient event
    cast the seed from whence came this reverent sentinel?

Was it a yearly flood
    of ages gone that no longer now occurs?
    Perhaps some ancestral kin covered the seed
    while seeking shelter from a storm
    or just some lowly furry form
    that saved a meal for future hungers' fill.

What changes
    have those boughs observed as man progressed about?

Time was,
    her sisters closely stood so thick
    that sun ne'er touched the ground,
    and now she stands alone.
    Then the peaceful silence was broken only by bird and wind
    and today she must endure man's machines' incessant moan.

I pledge to thee,
    my ancient friend, to make you proud of effort hence.

With this bough
    torn from you by the storm and cast upon the earth,
    shall I, with skills of ancient kin, create a life again.
    With loving heart, will I caress this gift
    and from it form for you an apology
    for my forefathers' thoughtlessness.

With tools
    honed sharp and practiced eye,
    I will make a shape to show
    your silent inner beauty of perfect grain
    and color shade—
    and with each caring, loving stroke,

A prayer for forgiveness
    from your majesty will be made.

—S. Gary Roberts

INTRODUCTION

This project book is intended to encourage, challenge, and enhance the reader's knowledge of woodturning as a skill. It is assumed that the woodturner will have basic knowledge and experience at the lathe. There have been many good books on turning that address in great detail the skills of tool sharpening, metal tempering, and grinding. I leave the teaching of those skills to those who are best qualified. These projects include spindle-turning, open bowls, and lidded boxes. From these three basic techniques all other woodturning procedures are derived. In this book, I deal with how the design of each project is used as a guide and how you can build and enjoy creating the projects.

Each project is narrated from start to finish and accompanied with dimensional drawings that will help lead the woodturner through the process. Suggestions are made on everything from project woods, in some instances, to finishes that take only a few moments.

LATHE SAFETY GUIDELINES

The following guidelines are reprinted with permission from the *1998 Resource Directory* of the American Association of Woodturners.

1. Safe, effective use of a wood lathe requires study and knowledge of procedures for using this tool. Read and thoroughly understand the label warnings on the lathe and in the owner/operator's manual.

2. Always wear safety goggles or safety glasses that include side protection and a full face shield when needed. Wood dust can be harmful to your respiratory system. Use a dust mask or helmet and proper ventilation (dust collection system) in dusty work conditions. Wear hearing protection during extended periods of operation.

3. Tie back long hair, and do not wear gloves, loose clothing, jewelry and/or any dangling objects that may catch in rotating parts or accessories.

4. Check the owner/operator's manual for proper speed recommendations. Use slower speeds for larger-diameter or rough pieces, and increased speed for smaller diameters and pieces that are balanced. If the lathe is shaking or vibrating, lower the speed. If the workpiece is vibrating, always stop the machine to check the reason.

5. Make certain that the belt guard or cover is in place. Check that all clamping devises (locks), such as on the tailstock and toolrest, are tight.

6. Rotate your workpiece by hand to make sure it clears the toolrest and bed before turning the lathe on. Be sure that the workpiece turns freely and is firmly mounted. It is always safest to turn the lathe off before adjusting the tool rest.

7. Exercise caution when using stock with any cracks, splits, checks, bark, knots, irregular shapes, or protuberances.

8. Hold turning tools securely on the toolrest, and also hold the tool in a controlled but comfortable manner. Always use a slower speed when starting until the workpiece is balanced. This helps avoid the possibility of an unbalanced piece jumping out of the lathe and striking the operator.

9. When running a lathe in reverse, it is possible for a chuck or faceplate to unscrew unless it is securely tightened on the lathe spindle.

10. Know your capabilities and your limits. An experienced woodturner may be capable of certain techniques and procedures that are not recommended for beginning turners.

11. When using a faceplate, be certain the workpiece is solidly mounted. When turning between centers, be certain the workpiece is secure.

12. Always remove the toolrest before sanding or polishing operations.

13. Do not overreach; keep proper footing and balance at all times.

14. Keep your lathe in good repair. Check for damaged parts, alignment, binding of moving parts, and other conditions that may affect its operation.

15. Keep tools sharp and clean for better and safer performance. Don't force a dull tool. Don't use a tool for a purpose not intended. Keep tools out of reach of children.

16. Consider your work environment. Do not use the lathe in damp or wet locations. Do not use it in the presence of flammable liquids or gases. Keep your work area well lit.

17. Stay alert. Watch what you are doing, use common sense. Don't operate tools when you are tired, or under the influence of drugs or alcohol.

18. Guard against electric shock. Inspect electric cords for damage. Avoid the use of extension cords.

19. Remove chuck keys and adjusting wrenches. Form a habit of checking for these before switching on the lathe.

20. Never leave the lathe running unattended. Turn the power off. Do not leave the lathe until it comes to a complete stop.

SANDING SUGGESTIONS

As on any project, sanding is the true key to any finish. If a piece is sanded well, any finish that seals the wood will look good. If it has not been sanded properly, it will never look good regardless of the finish used. Wood is a strict disciplinarian. Anytime you do not pay proper respect to the details—particularly the sanding—the finish will scold you severely.

Start sanding with a grit that is course enough to quickly clean away any marks made by the previous process. Each type of wood and style of project presents a different problem. Use the sandpaper as you would a chisel, to form and shape.

Choosing a grit that is too fine to sand away the chisel marks or end-grain shadows will only result in wasted time and material. Some woods respond well to sanding while others stubbornly resist. When the wood does not respond quickly, go immediately to a coarser-grit paper and you will find the one that will be effective and efficient.

It is a good rule always to use the grits in sequence; never skip over grits in the sanding process. Sand carefully with each successively finer paper until the wood is polished and clear of scratches. Skipping over several grits usually produces a finish that contains polished scratches from the courser grits.

A good practice is to turn off the lathe between grits, wipe the dust away with a cloth, and check to see if the wood is ready for you to go to the next step. In every size from 180-grit and finer, you should turn off the lathe and hand sand—with the grain—until all cross-grain scratches are gone. This will dramatically improve the outcome in any project you do and any finish you apply. The few moments that are spent here in close observation will pay big dividends later. If you are sanding the inside of a vessel, stop between grits and carefully clean the area being worked. As coarser grit comes loose from the paper or cloth, it will remain inside and continue to make scratches even though you have changed to a finer-grit sandpaper, unless you clean it out. Always clean the dust and grit from the project before advancing to the next level.

Everyone is guilty of picking up a piece of sandpaper that is worn and trying to do one more project. This can only result in poor finishes or extra time spent in sanding with finer grits. New paper always cuts best and this is really not the place to be frugal.

Storing your sandpaper is always a problem. To keep the different grits separate and organized, use file folders from an office supply. Identify each folder with a large felt-tipped pen and then discipline yourself to keep the sandpaper in the proper folder. This not only keeps it dry and straight, it keeps the grains of grit from transferring to other sizes that can create those mysterious scratches that sometimes "just appear."

Sanding seems to be the least enjoyed process in the shop. Perhaps good organization and understanding the process will improve your confidence level and therefore the pleasure of the task.

Please, for your own protection and good health, always be sure to wear lung protection—and always wear proper eye protection.

The author at his lathe. "Enjoy turning!"

FINISHES

If you ask five turners what their favorite finishing process would be, you usually will get at least ten answers. With this in mind, I will tell you how I finish my woodturnings. Throughout woodworking history, finishes have been unique to the individual artist or craftsman. Some of these finishes have been so individualistic that they are recognized as signatures.

I have enormous respect for our ancestors who religiously dedicated themselves to concocting and applying their finishes. Secret ingredients mixed at hidden places were common. Some of this attitude exists today, and anyone who cares that much about how their product looks is going to produce a good finish. The real point is to care about the finishing process and be self-disciplined to assure that it is the best finish that you can produce.

I believe that the finishing process begins with the final cuts on the lathe. The sanding process must be done correctly and with knowledgeable dedication. The application of liquid sealers, coatings, and waxes of any choice

will look good if the preparation is of excellent quality.

In the last few years, I have used one finishing process on everything. After the piece is sanded, I coat the wood with Deft™ Clear Satin Liquid (available from Deft, Inc., 17451 Von Karman, Irvine, CA 92614, 1-800-544-3338). This is kept in a wide-mouth quart-size jar filled with about 2 inches of liquid at a time. I saw off enough of the handle of a good-quality 1½" brush to allow it to fit inside the jar with the lid in place. Added to the liquid is about 30 percent lacquer thinner. As the mixture thickens over a period of time, more thinner is added. This process has these advantages: It dries almost instantly so that repeated coats can be done in a matter of minutes. The additional thinner not only speeds the drying process, it increases penetration and makes the product go further. All of these are good things. With the brush in the jar with the lid sealed, it is instantly accessible, and I rarely ever have to clean the brush. Well, once a year, I clean the brush whether it needs it or not.

Approach this procedure with caution, as experience is necessary. The first wheel uses Tripoli™ buffing compound. The second wheel uses the finer White Diamond™ compound, and the third and final wheel uses carnauba wax. All compounds are applied to the wheel while it is running. Apply the compound just before you buff the piece to be polished. I keep the wheels in separate plastic bags to eliminate the possibility of one grits transferring to another wheel. This also keeps them from being polluted with foreign particles.

Even cautious buffing can be accomplished in only moments. This buffing process will take almost any finish to a much higher level than can be achieved by most other methods.

LATHE INDEXING

The word "indexing" to many turners carries a rather mystically complex connotation that makes them recoil at the thought. With built-in index heads that have you counting holes and looking up owner's manuals, their reaction is certainly understandable. This is, however, a part of turning, and knowing how to approach the procedure will remove the mystery and replace it with the pleasure of knowledge. Here is a shop-made system that is very accurate, costs only a few cents to build, and is remarkably easy to use.

❖ For basic indexing, the circle contains 360 degrees from start to finish. Halfway around would be 360 degrees divided by two—or 180 degrees. One fourth of the circle would be 360 degrees divided by four—or 90 degrees—and so on. You must decide how many segments are appropriate for your project. Remember that the segments will always be equal parts of the 360-degree circle. You can divide the circle into as many segments as you wish, but they must be equal to end up at the same point that you started (360 degrees divided by the number of segments equals the degrees per segment). If we have a project on the lathe that requires that we divide it into segments, all we have to do is a little math and we know the number of degrees in each segment.

The method used I refer to as the "wet-and-wipe method." I wet the wood down quickly until it is soaked and the Deft™ starts running off. I immediately wipe it down with a lint-free cloth, rubbing briskly until it is dry, which takes only a few moments. The second coat is applied the same way, and occasionally on some wood a third coat is necessary. The wood will tell you how you are doing.

I let the piece dry a few minutes while I set up the Beall™ Buffing System (available from Beall Tool Co., 541 Swans Rd. NE, Newark, OH 43055, 1-800-331-4718, www.bealltool.com, email: jrbeall@bealltool.com). This system uses three buffing wheels. Insert a Jacobs chuck in the headstock and use a speed of 1,500 to 1,700 rpm. The cloth buffing wheel comes mounted on a ⅜" spindle that can be locked into the chuck. Be careful while buffing around the edges. The wheel can easily jerk the piece from your hand and ruin your piece—and your day.

❖ The next problem is how we transfer this information to the piece on the lathe. I have no quarrel with the built-in indexes because they work fine when you use them correctly. I prefer to use a compass to draw a circle on a piece of lightweight cardboard about the size of the handwheel. An empty cereal box works well for material.

❖ Calculate the number of degrees per segment and use a ruler or straightedge and draw a line from the pinpoint left by the compass in the center of the circle to any point on the edge of the circle. This point is both 0 degrees and 360 degrees. Use a protractor to divide the circle into as many segments as the project requires. A plastic protractor from the discount store works well for most projects. Get the kind that has a hole in the center for lining up the pinpoint in the center—this kind is easy to use and inexpensive.

❖ Mark off the degrees on the edge of the circle that you have drawn. Use the straightedge to divide off the segments. Make a note on the cardboard of the degrees that you calculated per segment. That way you can use it the next time you need that number of segments. If you have an even number of segments, you only have to calibrate half of the circle. When you mark off the half of the circle, lay your straightedge through the center pin mark to the other side and you can mark the other half at the same time.

❖ Cut the circle out of the cardboard with a pair of scissors. Glue a cork that will fit the hole in the center of the handwheel to the back of the cardboard circle. I use C/A (cyanoacrylate) glue for this purpose. A couple of small patches of double-stick carpet tape applied to the surface of the handwheel will keep the cardboard circle from slipping. Place a block of wood on the floor. Drill and insert a ⅜"- to ½"-dowel vertically long enough to reach up past the center of the lathe shaft.

❖ The last piece of this not-so-high-tech, shop-made indexing system is a wooden clothespin with a small screw pointing out of one side of the handle to act as an indicator. Place the clothespin on the dowel so that it is vertically near the center of the lathe shaft. Locate the point of the screw in the clothespin at the first line on the outer edge of the index wheel and you have the start.

❖ Adjust the tool rest to the center shaft level and mark the work piece along the top edge of the tool rest. Rotate the handwheel until the next line comes up to the clothespin pointer and mark the second line above the tool rest. Continue this process until you reach the point of beginning.

The rest of this procedure is repetitious unless you kick the block on the floor. (I hate it when I kick the block!) If you do have this happen, just go back to the last line at the tool rest and readjust the clothespin to be on any line at the edge of the index wheel, and finish the procedure. Enjoy turning!

MESQUITE VESSEL

This lidded bowl is made of Texas mesquite from the San Antonio area. This area produces an orange-colored mesquite. Experienced mesquite experts can tell which area of Texas produced the wood simply by its color. Various minerals in the soil and the climate affect the color and graining.

My grandfather, John Willis Roberts, hated mesquite. He spent his life fighting to keep it from coming back in his West Texas pastures. The young mesquite plants are covered in long toxic thorns that injure horses and cattle. He did,

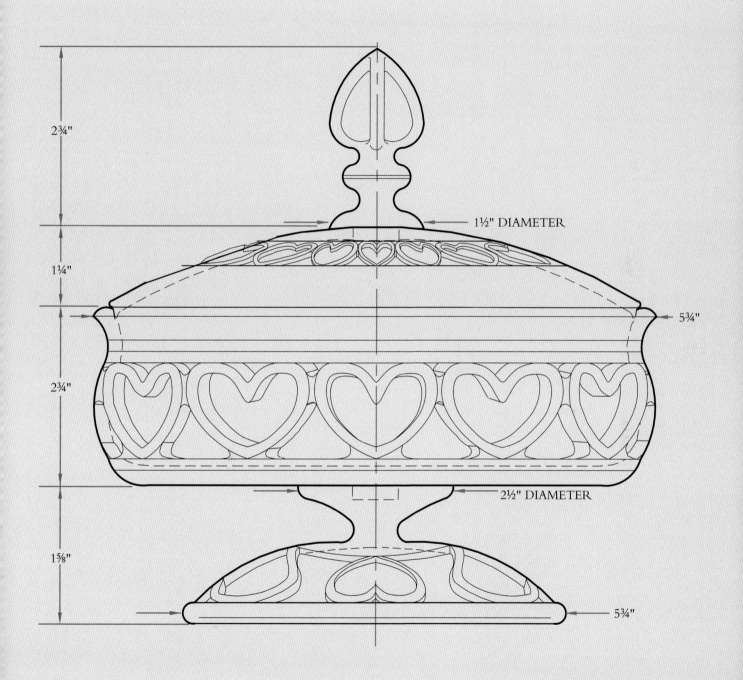

2¾"

1½" DIAMETER

1¼"

5¾"

2¾"

2½" DIAMETER

1⅝"

5¾"

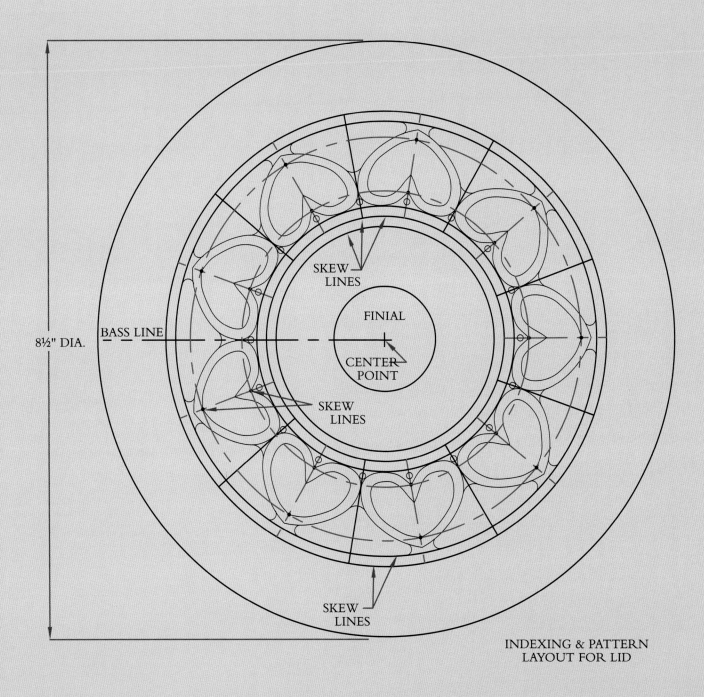

8½" DIA.

BASS LINE

SKEW LINES

FINIAL

CENTER POINT

SKEW LINES

SKEW LINES

INDEXING & PATTERN
LAYOUT FOR LID

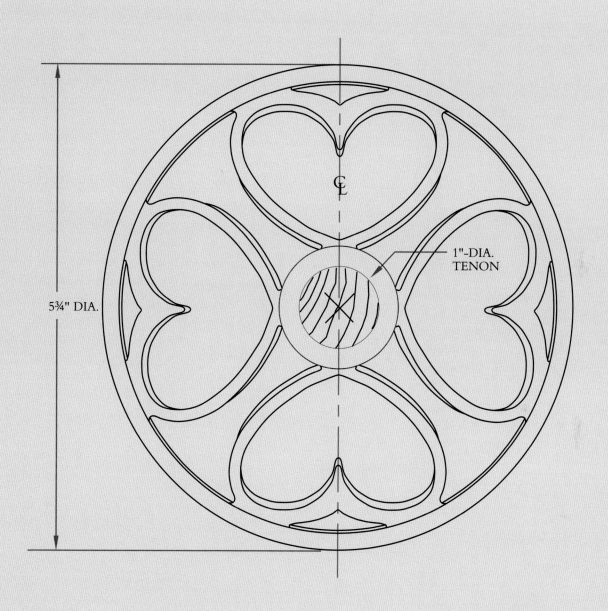

C
L

1"-DIA.
TENON

5¾" DIA.

PATTERN FOR BASE

A WONDERFUL WOOD—

My first remembrance of there being different kinds of woods was in my grandfather's shop. He would let me "help" him in his well-equipped farm shop, where he did everything from carpentry to blacksmithing.

One day he was making a singletree, to be used for pulling the horse-drawn wagon, out of a mesquite limb. My chore was to help with the clamps and pick up the chips. This was probably his way of keeping a boy busy and making him feel like he was helping his grandfather. The wood had heavy bark, a honey-colored center, and bright yellow sapwood. The chips were to be saved in a separate container and taken to the smoke house to be used later when we cured our meat.

I was curious about the use of freshly cut wood. His answer was that if you are going to make something of mesquite you have to make it while it is green. Otherwise, the wood will be too hard to cut with a drawknife. Besides, mesquite can be worked green with less chance than other woods of warping or splitting as it dries.

Once, I asked my grandfather if it would make a good house. He laughed and said that it did not get big enough but made the best singletrees, tool handles, and fuel for the smoke house. He pointed out the beauty, color, and graining, saying that any tree as bad as mesquite out on the range must have at least a few good qualities.

I have since found that mesquite is a wonderful wood for turning and carving. It has exceptional lateral grain strength.

Studies at Texas A & I University by Drs. Peter Felker and Mark Sorensen have indicated a wood with remarkable assets.

however, leave a small stand of mature trees near the house to be used for wooden handles and in the smoke house. I know he would be surprised that I like the wood and love working it.

Some of the findings by researchers at Texas A & I University (see the sidebar to the right on page 17 for more) include that its volumetric shrinkage and swelling are far less than those of other fine hardwoods: 16.1% and 13.6% for red oak and pecan, respectively, but only 4.7% for mesquite. Perhaps more importantly, mesquite's radial and tangential shrinkages are nearly identical, which means that when it does shrink or swell, it does so in the same amount in both directions. This is why it is so unlikely to crack or warp as it dries, after being worked reasonably thin. End-grain sealing seems to be effective for storing thicker pieces.

Selecting Your Piece

When you are selecting a piece of mesquite for turning, you should be aware that the shape and thickness will affect the visual result of carved-through patterns. Inconsistencies in wall thickness will distort the shape of the designs to be carved. Careful measuring of wall thickness with a figure-eight caliper is essential. Also, carving around a bead or cove adds to the complexity. Simple configuration and nearly level planes work the easiest and produce the best results.

Working on the Lathe

In all lathe procedures, I use the tailstock to support the piece for as long as possible. This increases safety and quality. Turn the body on a faceplate. The lid, base and finial are turned between centers. Use a deep-Vee bowl gouge. No other special tools are required or used for this turning project. Delineating the area to be carved with a couple of skew lines frames the carving. The lines act as stop cuts during carving. Shallow mortise-and-tenon construction throughout keeps the pieces centered during assembly.

I like "running" patterns, which repeat around a turning. Differences in diameter, however, can dramatically affect and distort the intended concept. Planning and drawing are critical to this type of project. A pencil is the most important tool in your shop and should be the most frequently used. I use full-size drawings and apply them directly to the piece. Before removing the piece from the lathe, I use a shop-made index, detailed earlier on pages 10 and 11, to check and see how the pattern will lay out on the piece. If design modifications are necessary, this is the time to see if they will work and how they will actually look.

Finishing

Achieving a smooth, sanded finish on pierced carvings is a challenge to both patience and ingenuity. I use power anytime I can. I converted an old electric filleting knife into a power sander by adding double-stick tape to the stub end of its broken blade. I then applied sandpaper to the tape. It makes a fine sanding tool and can be modified by duct-taping various-sized dowels to the blade end. Apply double-stick tape to the dowels. Cloth-backed sandpaper sticks better to the tape than paper-backed.

I applied a coat of Deft™ to seal the wood. I then used drafting tape to draw and carve the pattern. Drafting tape does not leave an adhesive residue like masking tape. It is available at most office supply stores. Leave the tape in place and carve through the pattern.

I finished this project as I do most others by using liquid clear satin Deft™ thinned 30% with lacquer thinner. I apply a dripping wet coat and wipe down with a lint-free cloth. Two or three coats are usually sufficient. Between coats, instead of fine steel wool, I find that commercially available plastic abrasive scrubber pads work better. They do not leave fine steel particles in the wood and give a better finish. After curing time, I buff the accessible areas with a Beall™ Buffing System mounted in the headstock of the lathe. I use about 2,000 rpm. Be especially careful around the carved areas. Last, I usually apply a hand-rubbed coat of paste wax. I like the feel and finish the wax gives. This also helps, if the project is to be handled at a demonstration or show, to keep fingerprints to a minimum.

I think you will enjoy turning with mesquite; the first nine projects have been turned in this wonderful wood, and others suggest its use.

MESQUITE LUMBER—

In "Understanding Mesquite Lumber," a paper by Peter Felker and Mark Sorensen (available from the Center for Semi-Arid Forest Resources, Texas A & I University, Kingsville, TX 78363), we find this analysis:

"Mesquite's hard wood makes it ideal for furniture and flooring applications. For example, the force required to push one-half the diameter of a $7/16$" steel ball into a piece of plain-sawed wood was 690 lbs. for loblolly pine, 1,450 lbs. for sugar maple, 1,060 lbs. for red oak and 2,340 lbs. for mesquite (Texas Forest Products Lab #140, 1986). This hardness makes it possible to sand the wood for a natural high polish. Mesquite wood is easy to sand since the wood does not contain oils that clog up sandpaper.

"Due to the adverse conditions under which mesquite grows, the trees seldom reach heights of 35 feet, and they branch low to the ground. As a result, logs for mesquite are typically short (3 to 6 feet), small in diameter (less than 18 inches), twisted, and have a radial crack that runs the length of the log. In some hardwood tree species, highly figured grain patterns are generally restricted to the interface where the trunk and root system meet. In contrast, many of the aboveground portions of mesquite have considerable figure. Unfortunately, many of these highly figured pieces are also associated with knotholes and cracks. Fortunately these holes can be very attractively filled with a clear casting resin.

"The heartwood of mesquite is light brown or pink when freshly cut but eventually darkens to a dark orange–red with age. The sapwood of mesquite is yellow, and is not very dimensionally stable."

2 VINY MESQUITE DECANTER

Mesquite is my favorite wood for turning vessels of this type. It has excellent lateral-grain strength, carves well, and gives a beautiful natural grain finish (see pages 16–17).

I use only dead wood in my work, aiming to give a new life and form to what was once a natural beauty. The log that produced this product was heading for a campfire when I rescued it from some mildly amused campers.

The procedures used in making this vessel are typical of those used to make any vessel that requires hollowing from the bottom. This method was developed by Dale Nish of Provo, Utah, and presented at the annual symposium held at Brigham Young University.

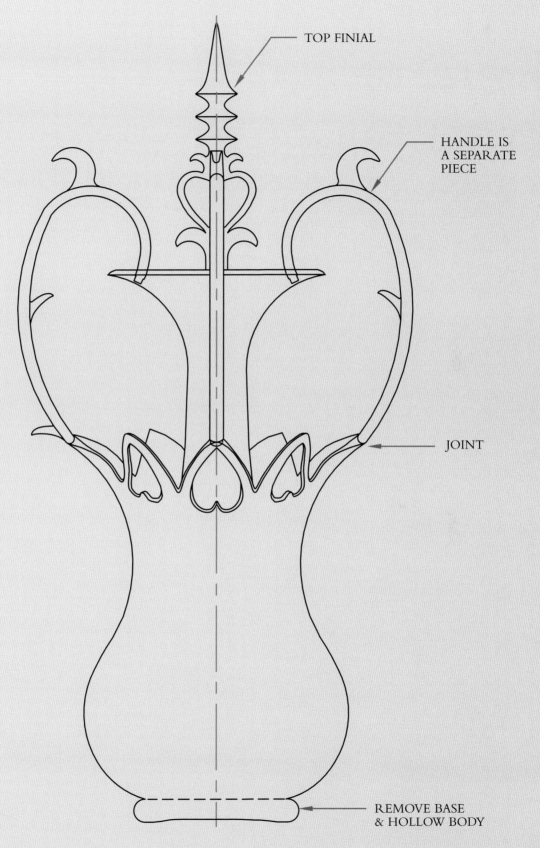

TOP FINIAL

HANDLE IS
A SEPARATE
PIECE

JOINT

REMOVE BASE
& HOLLOW BODY

19

TURNING A CARVED DECANTER

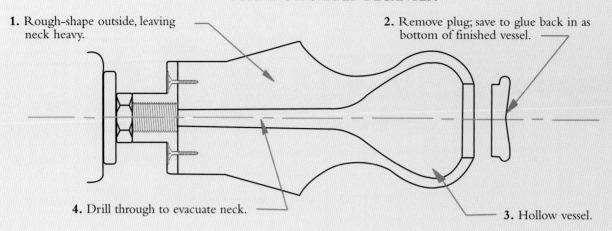

1. Rough-shape outside, leaving neck heavy.

2. Remove plug; save to glue back in as bottom of finished vessel.

4. Drill through to evacuate neck.

3. Hollow vessel.

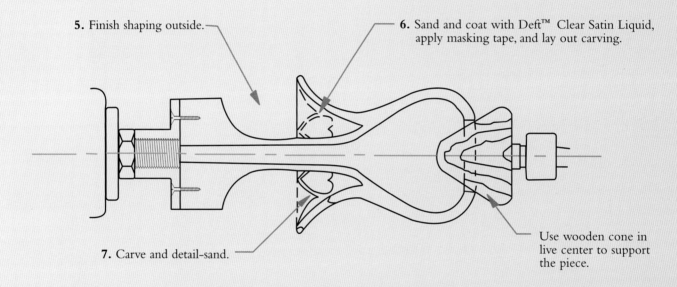

5. Finish shaping outside.

6. Sand and coat with Deft™ Clear Satin Liquid, apply masking tape, and lay out carving.

7. Carve and detail-sand.

Use wooden cone in live center to support the piece.

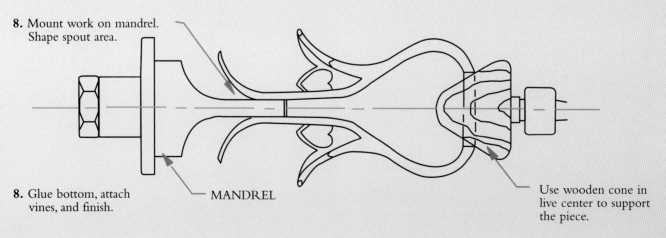

8. Mount work on mandrel. Shape spout area.

8. Glue bottom, attach vines, and finish.

MANDREL

Use wooden cone in live center to support the piece.

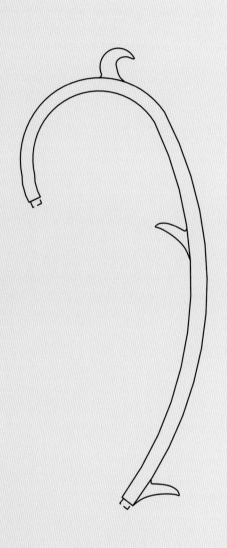

"VINE" HANDLE PATTERN   FINIAL PATTERN

1. Mount a suitable-size turning blank on a 3" faceplate. Make sure that the screws are in solid wood and that the blank is securely attached to the faceplate. Bring up the tailstock with a cup-and-pin live center to support the piece while you turn it into a balanced cylinder. You should always keep safety in mind and use the tailstock in your project whenever possible.

SPEAKING OF SAFETY—

When you are turning you should always wear eye and lung protection. Do not use a high pressure air hose to blow dust from your clothes. This can cause serious injury if you happen to pass over bare skin or your face. I wear a glove on the hand near the tool rest when turning wood that has bark and pieces of wood that could come partially loose and injure the hand before it can be moved away. Otherwise, it is dangerous to wear gloves while turning.

Remember to wear a dust mask even when cleaning the shop.

2. And now, with safety in mind, back to the project. With the tailstock removed, turn, finish, and remove from the bottom of the piece the plug that will become the base later. Drill a hole through to the faceplate. Now you can hollow the base of the turning and fit the plug as you would in a lidded box. Lay the base aside to be glued in place later.
3. Do not remove all the wood from the upper body and neck area until you have the inside excavated. It is not necessary to sand the inside of the body. Using a cone-type live center, bring up the tailstock to support the piece while shaping the neck and flange that will later be carved. Finish sanding and apply a coat of sealer before shaping the top.
4. Remove the piece from the faceplate and make a new faceplate mounted mandrel to fit the drilled hole. Using the cone live center and the mandrel, you can finish the top and still have the project perfectly centered. Be cautious about using too much pressure on the cone or you can split the turning.
5. Once the piece is turned, sanded, and sealed, you can cover the area to be carved with drafting tape. This will allow you to make pencil marks on a surface that can be easily removed. I use the shop made indexing system detailed earlier in this book to lay out both horizontal and vertical lines for the pattern to be carved.

I carve through the tape using a shop-made carving knife that has a short, stout blade ¾" long. I detail and finish-sand the carved area with a reversible, variable, high-speed mini-grinder (I prefer the Optima II™, see pages 26, 112, 117, and 123 for some sources). The small handpiece and flexible cord provide ample power and ease of control without tiring the hand. A small ⅛" split mandrel that holds scraps of cloth-backed sandpaper makes an excellent flap sander to get into the tight places. Be sure to wear a quality dust mask and eye protection. Tiny pieces of grit thrown from the sandpaper can do serious damage to unprotected eyes.

I pattern out the "vine" handles in scrap wood, then cut them out on a scroll saw. Joining the pieces to the turning takes a lot of care. A bad joint can really ruin the effect. I cut the surfaces to be joined at a 45-degree angle, then glue them with C/A (cyanoacrylate) glue. Next, hand-shape the transition joint until the two parts flow into one another. (For more on handles, see the next project, number 4, the "Mesquite Twister.")

In designing a finial for a project such as this, I like to emulate the design of the body by doing some carving on the top. It just adds to the overall quality of the finished turning.

Finishes I like best are those that give a quality grain enhancement and do not consume a lot of time. See "Sanding Suggestions" and "Finishes" in the Introduction, pages 8, 9, and 10.

Assembly is done after the finish is applied, and requires some care in gluing. Be careful to eliminate any excess glue before it dries and creates more hand work.

Once finished, I use a Dremel™ engraver to sign and date the piece, and identify the wood. This should answer most questions by admirers—except "How long did this take?"

3

BY THE NUMBERS

I want to share with you a project that changed the way that I approach designing a piece. In June 1993, the editor of the *North Carolina Woodturner,* Ken Bachand, published an article by Tony Bradley, "An Introduction to Proportion."

In this article, Mr. Bradley converted the "golden rectangle" (in which the width is to the length as the length is to their sum) into a mathematical equation that I suddenly understood, which made it possible for me to design a project mathematically as it progressed. This project is the result of Tony Bradley's concept and his sharing with all turners.

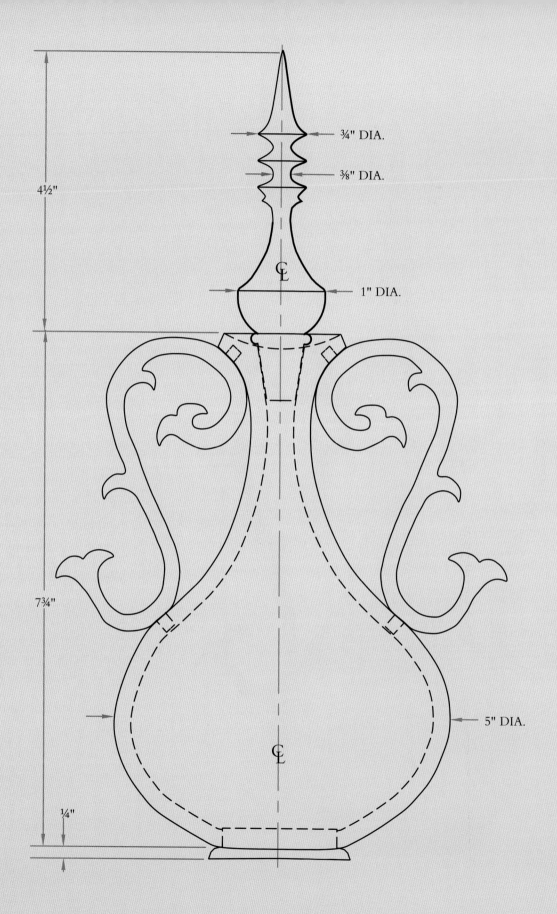

¾" DIA.

⅜" DIA.

1" DIA.

4½"

7¾"

¼"

5" DIA.

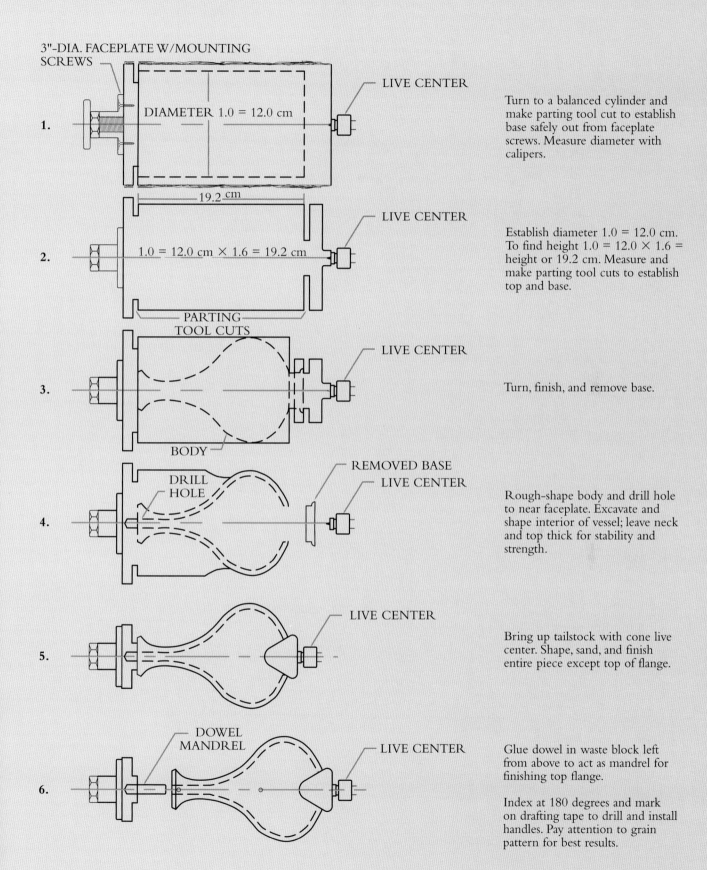

3"-DIA. FACEPLATE W/MOUNTING SCREWS

1. DIAMETER 1.0 = 12.0 cm — LIVE CENTER

Turn to a balanced cylinder and make parting tool cut to establish base safely out from faceplate screws. Measure diameter with calipers.

2. 19.2 cm — 1.0 = 12.0 cm × 1.6 = 19.2 cm — LIVE CENTER

Establish diameter 1.0 = 12.0 cm. To find height 1.0 = 12.0 × 1.6 = height or 19.2 cm. Measure and make parting tool cuts to establish top and base.

3. PARTING TOOL CUTS — LIVE CENTER — BODY

Turn, finish, and remove base.

4. DRILL HOLE — REMOVED BASE — LIVE CENTER

Rough-shape body and drill hole to near faceplate. Excavate and shape interior of vessel; leave neck and top thick for stability and strength.

5. LIVE CENTER

Bring up tailstock with cone live center. Shape, sand, and finish entire piece except top of flange.

6. DOWEL MANDREL — LIVE CENTER

Glue dowel in waste block left from above to act as mandrel for finishing top flange.

Index at 180 degrees and mark on drafting tape to drill and install handles. Pay attention to grain pattern for best results.

25

"GOLDEN RECTANGLE"—

You can use the proportions of the "golden rectangle," which originated with the ancient Greeks and has for centuries been regarded as the key to the mysteries of art, in the design of your turned vessels. In his article, Tony Bradley converted the "golden rectangle" proportion, in which the width is to the length as the length is to their sum, by converting the close ratio of 5 to 8 to the decimal equivalent with a relationship of 1.0 to 1.6. Thus, For each 1.0 unit of diameter, use 1.6 units of height. In a horizontal-silhouette vessel, use 1.6 units of width for every 1.0 unit of height. Now, you can measure and mathematically calculate one dimension in relation to the other. This allows you to design your project on paper before you go to the lathe.

Note: For vertical pieces always multiply the maximum diameter by 1.6 to get the height. For horizontal pieces always divide the diameter by 1.6 then multiply by 1.0 to get the height.

THE "ONE-THIRD–TWO-THIRDS" RULE

Once I had the height and diameter, I could begin to establish the other relationships using the "one-third–two-thirds" rule. I felt that the base should be about ⅔ of the diameter of the body and that the upper flange should be about ⅓ of the same dimension. In this kind of figuring I find that using metric units makes the computation simple and convenient. (See page 160 for a useful chart of approximate metric equivalents and conversion factors.)

Using the Proportion

1. Taking Bradley's concept, I mounted a mesquite log on a 3" faceplate in the lathe and brought up the tailstock with a cup-and-pin live center to support the piece.

2. I rough-turned the log to a balanced cylinder and with a pair of calipers measured the diameter. Because this was going to be a vertical vessel, the diameter would be the smaller of the two relations (i.e., 1.0). I could take that dimension, converted to metric for ease of computation, and know what the height (1.6) should be. In this instance, the diameter was 12.0 cm. To get the height, use the ratio of 1.0 = 12.0 cm by 1.6 = 19.2 cm.

3. Applying the "one-third–two-thirds" rule, I turned the base down to 8 cm (⅔ of the 12-cm diameter), shaped, finished, and parted off the base, leaving a tenon to be glued in later. This allowed access for hollowing through the bottom. The base should fit back into the body like a lidded box, so use calipers and make sure it fits snugly.

4. Using the tailstock with a drill chuck, drill a hole past the mark that indicates the top of the vessel. Choose a bit size that will be large enough to accept the finial tenon later. If your drill bit is not long enough, drill as deep as you can, then wait until you have excavated a portion of the material from inside the body. You will then be able to run the bit and chuck into the hole to complete that procedure.

5. Shape the outside of the body, but leave the neck thick enough to support the piece. I use a Dennis Stewart hollowing system, (available from Craft Supplies USA, Provo, UT 84606, 1-800-551-8876, www.woodturnerscatalog.com). The chisel has a small ⅛" point. This excavates the wood quickly and gives excellent control.

    Using figure-eight calipers to check the wall thickness, it is not difficult to taper the body wall to meet the drilled hole. You do not have to sand inside.

6. Once the body is excavated, bring up the tailstock with a cone on the live center to support the piece. There are several well-made cone-type live-center systems on the market. However, if you do not have one, you can easily turn one that will work on this project as well as many others. Make sure you do not exert too much pressure on the cone as you can split the wood in the thin walls of the body.

7. You can now measure and make the top flange of the vessel. I wanted to use the diameter of the body as a guide and make it ⅓ of that diameter, or 4.0 cm. We have already established the height of the vessel, so you can simply set the calipers to 4.0 cm and turn the flange to that diameter.

8. Turn and finish the exterior of the piece. It is difficult to finish the top of the upper flange until you have parted it off of the faceplate. To solve this problem, drill a hole into the waste left on the faceplate and insert a dowel the size of the hole drilled for the finial. This will serve as a mandrel and allow you to finish the top of the flange.

Designing the Finial and Handles

The same 1.0-to-1.6 relationship can be incorporated into the design of the finial. The finial should be visually compatible with and similar in design to the body of the vessel. Be sure to turn the tenon that fits into the drilled hole long enough to be stable. Taper the tenon slightly larger than the hole. It should fit like a cork to be impressive.

Handles are also a part of the design equation. I try to make the handles about ⅔ of the height of the vessel. Their width should be about ⅓ the overall diameter. This, of course, depends on the shape of the piece to which they are to be attached and on whether they are to be vinelike, free-form, or geometric. This is my personal preference but handles can add great value and beauty to an otherwise ordinary turning.

I suggest that you do several sketches of handles before you make your final decision for a design. Two pencils taped together is an easy way to draw parallel lines. Cut out a paper pattern of the handle and tape them to the piece before you cut out the wood. You may find, in looking at them, that you want to modify the shape. It is much easier to modify while still in paper form.

Cut out the pattern with a scroll saw. I use a reversible variable-speed mini-grinder to finish the shaping and sanding. A variety of burrs, sanding drums, and split-mandrel flap sanders are available from most carving supply stores for the mini-grinders. I do not hesitate to use power tools when they will do the job efficiently.

Tenons that hold the handles to the body tend to be weak because of their size. Before mounting, drill a small hole in the hidden end of the tenon and insert a brass pin to prevent breakage.

See "Sanding Suggestions" and "Finishes" earlier on pages 8, 9, and 10.

Finished and buffed, the assembly should be done with care minimizing the use of glue to prevent runs. You will find that with buffed and waxed surfaces, cleanup is not too difficult, should it be necessary.

FINDING WHAT YOU NEED

Mesquite is not always something that is easy to come by in other regions. Here is a good source to try:

Unique Mesquite   www.woodfinder.net
Harold Jambers, Jr.   830-256-4414
499 Jambers Ranch Rd.
Whitsett, TX 78075
email: arrowj3@awsomenet.net

Throughout this project, I kept thinking that without the education, information, and fellowship created by the American Association of Woodturners, this turning would not have been possible.

If you are not now a member of this fine association that is "dedicated to providing education, information and organization to those interested in woodturning," their address is: 222 Landmark Center, 75 West Fifth Street, St. Paul, MN 55102, ph: 651-484-9094, fax: 651-484-1724, inquires@woodturner.org, www.woodturner.org

Supplies are available from many sources, including your local craft store and mail-order catalogues. See also pages 51, 112, 117, and 123 for a few suggestions.

4

MESQUITE TWISTER

This piece was turned from Texas mesquite rescued from a barbecue woodpile. The design was inspired by the whirlwinds that wander the hot summer prairies and torment the enduring mesquite trees they encounter.

The bottom was removed as narrated in the two previous projects, Numbers 2 and 3; so in this description the concentration will be on the handles.

The design was carefully conceived and then drawn with the intent that the handles would be carved out of quarter-sawed wood for lateral-grain strength and then twisted along the axis to give the 90-degree warp from bottom to top.

29

HANDLE PATTERN

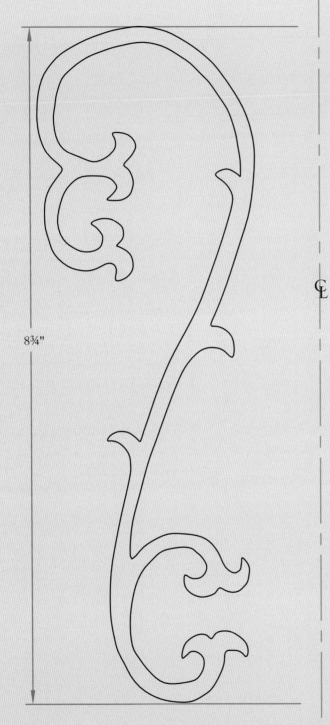

8¾"

C̶L

HANDLE PATTERN
AFTER BENDING

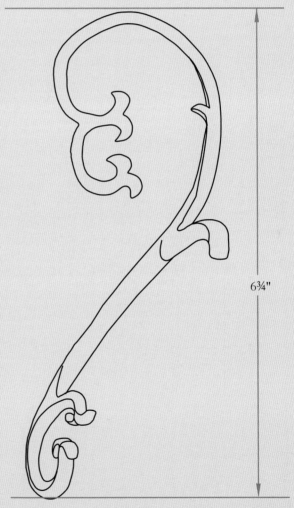

6¾"

FINIAL TURNING SEQUENCE

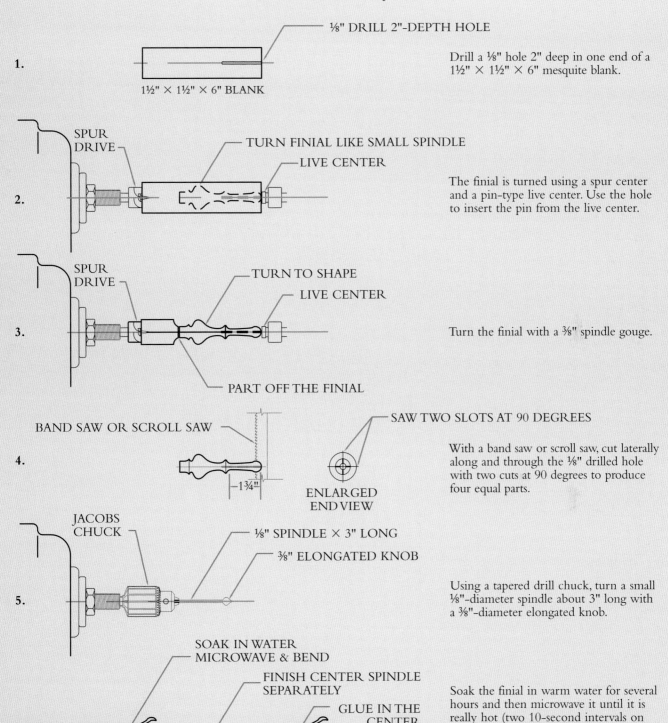

1.

⅛" DRILL 2"-DEPTH HOLE

1½" × 1½" × 6" BLANK

Drill a ⅛" hole 2" deep in one end of a 1½" × 1½" × 6" mesquite blank.

2.

SPUR DRIVE

TURN FINIAL LIKE SMALL SPINDLE

LIVE CENTER

The finial is turned using a spur center and a pin-type live center. Use the hole to insert the pin from the live center.

3.

SPUR DRIVE

TURN TO SHAPE

LIVE CENTER

PART OFF THE FINIAL

Turn the finial with a ⅜" spindle gouge.

4.

BAND SAW OR SCROLL SAW

1¾"

SAW TWO SLOTS AT 90 DEGREES

ENLARGED END VIEW

With a band saw or scroll saw, cut laterally along and through the ⅛" drilled hole with two cuts at 90 degrees to produce four equal parts.

5.

JACOBS CHUCK

⅛" SPINDLE × 3" LONG

⅜" ELONGATED KNOB

Using a tapered drill chuck, turn a small ⅛"-diameter spindle about 3" long with a ⅜"-diameter elongated knob.

6.

SOAK IN WATER MICROWAVE & BEND

FINISH CENTER SPINDLE SEPARATELY

GLUE IN THE CENTER SPINDLE SHAFT

Soak the finial in warm water for several hours and then microwave it until it is really hot (two 10-second intervals on HIGH worked best.) With gloves on slowly bend the petals out, indent the area near the ends of the bent pieces, and install the shaft of the ⅛"-diameter spindle in the center hole with C/A glue.

BENDING MESQUITE—

I had heard and read descriptions of using heat and moisture to shape wood, but when I tried to duplicate the effort using mesquite, it ended in failure or breakage.

The plan was to heat the handles over steam from a pressure cooker. After breaking two handles scroll-sawed from green or fresh-cut mesquite, I concluded that I was not getting the pieces uniformly hot enough. Two other methods resulted in failure. The breakage seemed to result from having inconsistent thickness in the unfinished handle. To solve this, the trial handle was carved, sanded, and finished without a sealer. This was a substantial amount of effort to invest in a piece that if broken would have to be discarded, but I was determined to come up with a process that could be duplicated.

Finally, I decided to try soaking the completely carved handle in warm water for about an hour and then microwaving it until it was really hot. I found that two 10-second intervals on the high setting, the second period immediately following the first, worked best. The wood actually started crackling like bacon frying at the end of the second 10-second period. This seemed to be the best signal that it was time to stop. Too much heat can discolor the wood and even set it on fire.

With thick work gloves to protect the hands, I removed the hot piece from the oven and s-l-o-w-l-y twisted it to the desired shape. I then held the piece in place and ran cold tap water over the piece, hands, and gloves. It was like shaping metal. Once cooled, the handle retained its twisted shape. SUCCESS!! So there, mesquite!

For making the handles for the vessel, see the sidebar "Bending Mesquite."

❖ The twisted handles were hung in the shop for a day to air dry before sanding and finishing.

❖ I turned a 3/16" dowel out of the same wood to act as a pin to fasten the lower part of the handle to the body. The upper part of the handle was designed to hook through a carved opening in the lip of the spout and is not fastened with pin or glue.

❖ The finial is turned using a spur center and pin-type live center. First, drill a 1/8" hole 2" deep in one end of a 1½" × 1½" × 6" blank. Use the hole to insert the pin from the live center. Turn the finial with a 3/8" spindle gouge—or your favorite chisel. Make the stopper or tenon end the correct size to fit into the drilled hole in the top of the vessel. A taper turned on the upper end of the tenon will make it fit like a cork.

❖ With a band saw or scroll saw, cut laterally along and through the 1/8" drilled hole at 90-degree angles to produce four equal quadrants.

❖ Using a chuck, turn a small 1/8" spindle about 3" long with an elongated knob on one end. This will be inserted in the drilled hole later to complete the finial. Since the wood of the finial is thicker than the handles, a longer soaking period is required. Leave it several hours before heating and bending as described in the sidebar.

❖ Use a high-speed, handheld mini-grinder and a small round ball burr to indent the bulged areas near the ends of the bent pieces. Install the shaft of the 1/8" spindle in the center hole. This will give the appearance that the center piece came from the finial. It is best to sand and finish these two pieces separately before gluing in the shaft.

When the finished piece was entered into a show, a longtime mesquite worker approached me and said he had heard that I told someone that I had steam-bent the handles. I informed him it was not really steam but rather moisture and heat. His comment was that was the same thing and mesquite could not be steamed and bent. I continued the debate by showing him the grain was straight and followed the twisted curve. He left grumbling that I must have found a crooked piece of wood and that no one could bend mesquite.

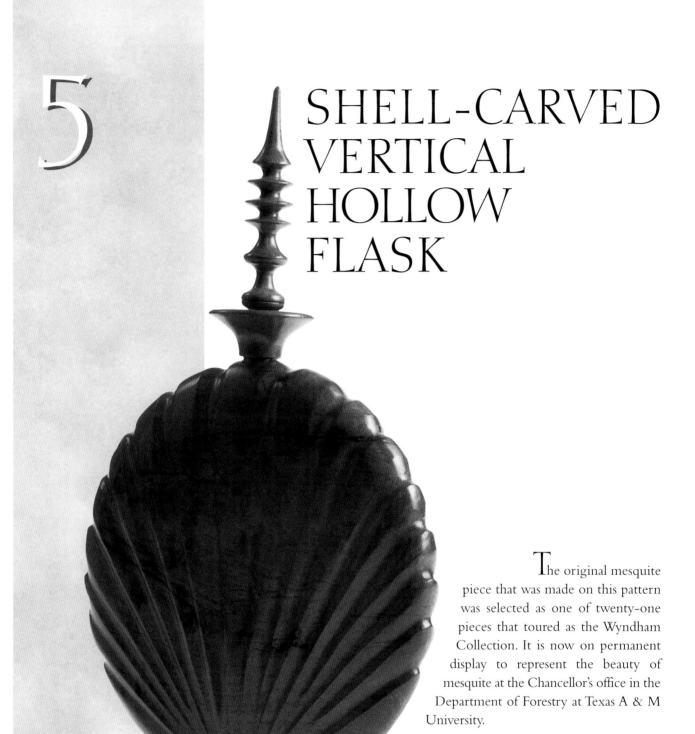

5 SHELL-CARVED VERTICAL HOLLOW FLASK

The original mesquite piece that was made on this pattern was selected as one of twenty-one pieces that toured as the Wyndham Collection. It is now on permanent display to represent the beauty of mesquite at the Chancellor's office in the Department of Forestry at Texas A & M University.

Making the Hollow Flask

The body of this project is made from two pieces of quarter-sawed wood that start out at 8" wide planed to 1" thickness and are then band-sawed to round.

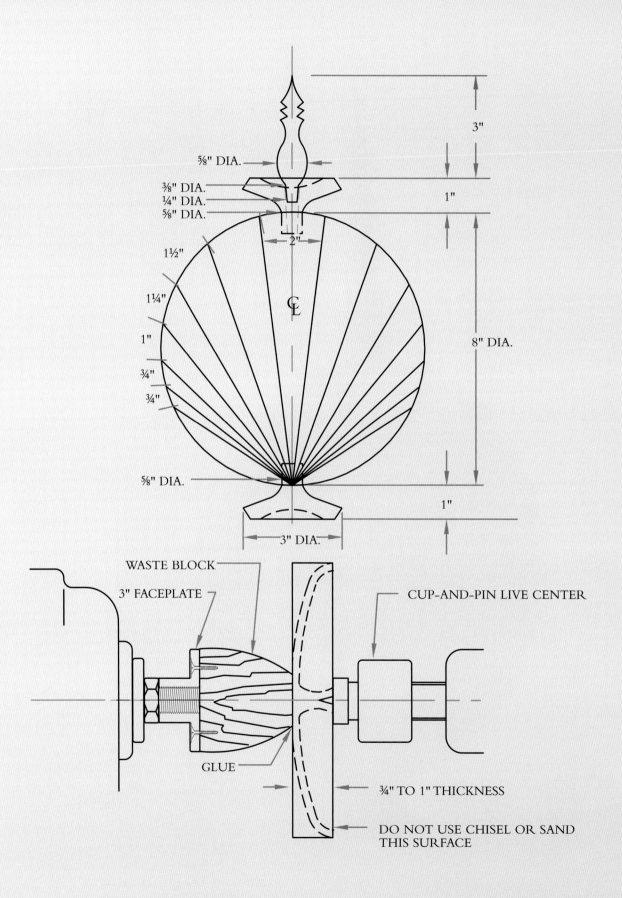

5/8" DIA.

3/8" DIA.
1/4" DIA.
5/8" DIA.

3"

1"

2"

1 1/2"

1 1/4"

1"

3/4"

3/4"

C̶L

8" DIA.

5/8" DIA.

1"

3" DIA.

WASTE BLOCK

3" FACEPLATE

CUP-AND-PIN LIVE CENTER

GLUE

3/4" TO 1" THICKNESS

DO NOT USE CHISEL OR SAND
THIS SURFACE

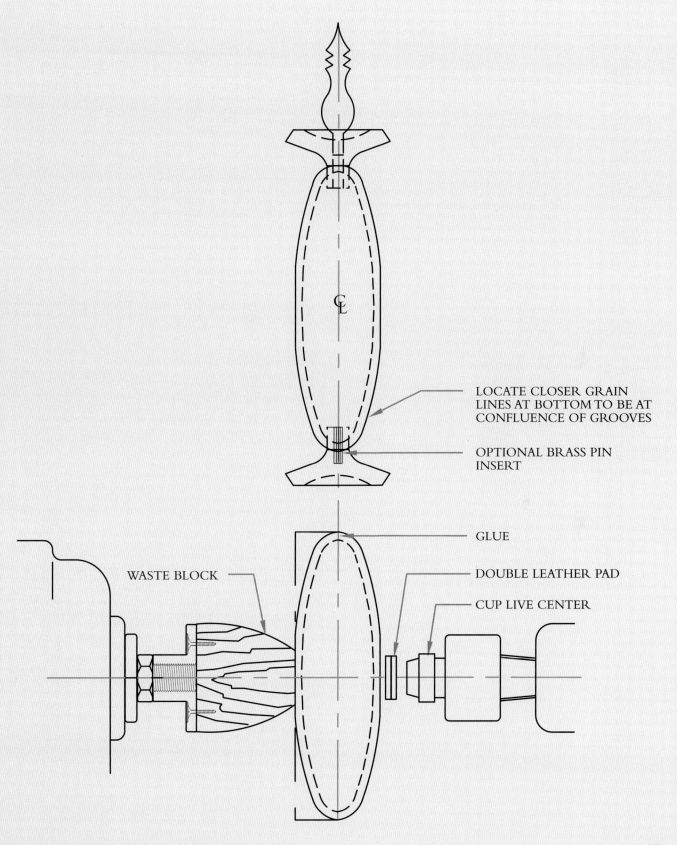

LOCATE CLOSER GRAIN
LINES AT BOTTOM TO BE AT
CONFLUENCE OF GROOVES

OPTIONAL BRASS PIN
INSERT

GLUE

WASTE BLOCK

DOUBLE LEATHER PAD

CUP LIVE CENTER

Turning the Body Pieces

1. On a 3" faceplate with a waste block turned down to 2" diameter, use C/A (cyanoacrylate) glue or double-stick carpet tape to adhere one-half of the body on to the waste block.

Bring up the tailstock with a cup-and-pin live center to secure the piece against the waste block. (See the drawings.)

2. Turn both sides with your favorite spindle gouge.
3. Use figure-eight calipers to obtain a consistent ³⁄₁₆" wall thickness. Take into consideration the loss of wall thickness for sanding.

There is no need to sand the inside (see "Sanding Suggestions" and "Finishing" earlier on pages 8, 9, and 10). Do not use a chisel or sandpaper on the planed surface edges—as they will act as the glue joint later.

4. Remove the first half from the lathe by parting away the waste block side of the glue joint and lay the turned piece aside for later use.
5. Turn the second half of the body. Make sure that the outside of the turning is from the same side of the board from which they came so that when put together, there will be a grain match on the edge.

Joining the Body Pieces

6. With the second half of the body still on the waste block, check the grain match and join the two pieces with C/A glue. The tailstock with a cup center will act as a clamp to hold the pieces together.

Use a double leather pad between the cup center and the piece to protect the wood. Be cautious not to exert too much pressure with the tailstock or you could crack the thin wood or distort the glue joint.

Smoothing the Glue Joint

7. When the glue dries, leave the live center in place and turn the glue joint smooth. There is usually excess glue and some distortion where the two pieces are joined. Carefully make light cuts. A catch here can ruin your day.

Separating the Body from the Lathe

8. Remove the body from the lathe and, using a pad sander, finish the area that was under the waste block.
9. Locate the closest grain lines at the confluence of the grooves, which on this project will be at the bottom of the flask. Drill holes in the top and bottom for the flange and foot.

These two holes will be on the centerline of the vessel and will be used to begin the indexing process as detailed in Project Number 23.

Carving the Shell Pattern

Use the same procedure in preparing the shell pattern for the flask as described in "Carving the Shell Pattern," for Project Number 23, on page 112. Remember the wall thickness—not too deep!

Making the Top Flange

The top flange is turned on a screw center or threaded-rod center as detailed in "Using a Threaded-Rod Center," in Project Number 10, on page 54. The base is turned on a four-jaw chuck or waste block.

Turning the Finial

The finial is turned between centers. Use a small ³⁄₈" spur center and cup-type live center. Use calipers to size the tenon that will fit into the top flange. Turn a slight taper on the upper side of the tenon so that the finial fits like a cork.

Strengthening the Base

On some woods, the ⁵⁄₈" tenon in the base could be too weak to support the turning. If this is the case, before assembly drill and glue in place a short length of ¹⁄₈"-diameter brass rod in the center of the tenon. This will show only on the inside and cannot be seen after the finished shell-carved vertical hollow flask has been assembled.

This striking piece is always admired for the graining display and the light weight when held.

6

ANOTHER BLOOMING MESQUITE

Indigenous people believed, it is commonly thought, that the circle is a sacred symbol and the sphere the sacred source and origin of all things. In this project, we find life, blooms, and leaves bursting from within the turned sphere.

These pieces were all made from the same log of mesquite that was cleared away to make room for agriculture. This project was dedicated to giving the wood a new life form, the beauty of which can barely approach that of the tree from which it came, but nevertheless reflects its life and conditions.

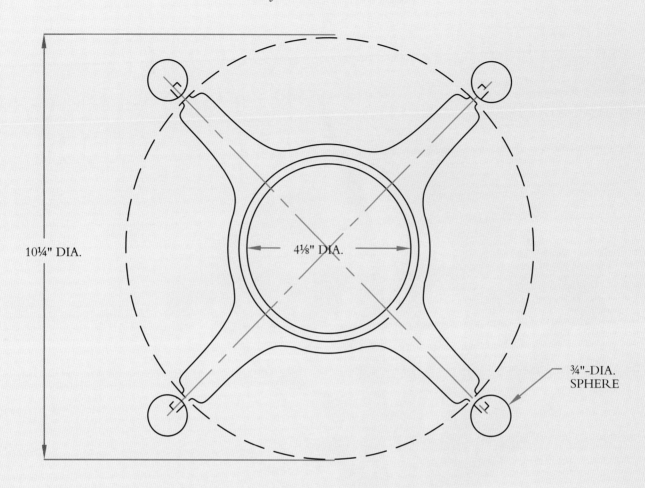

10¼" DIA.

4⅛" DIA.

¾"-DIA.
SPHERE

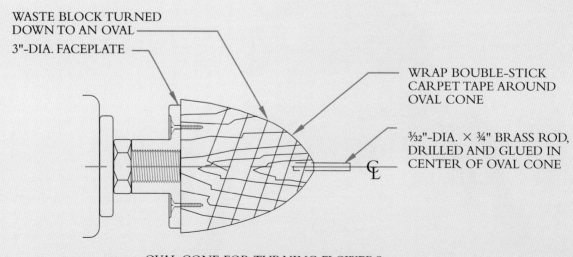

WASTE BLOCK TURNED
DOWN TO AN OVAL

3"-DIA. FACEPLATE

WRAP BOUBLE-STICK
CARPET TAPE AROUND
OVAL CONE

³⁄₃₂"-DIA. × ¾" BRASS ROD,
DRILLED AND GLUED IN
CENTER OF OVAL CONE

OVAL CONE FOR TURNING FLOWERS

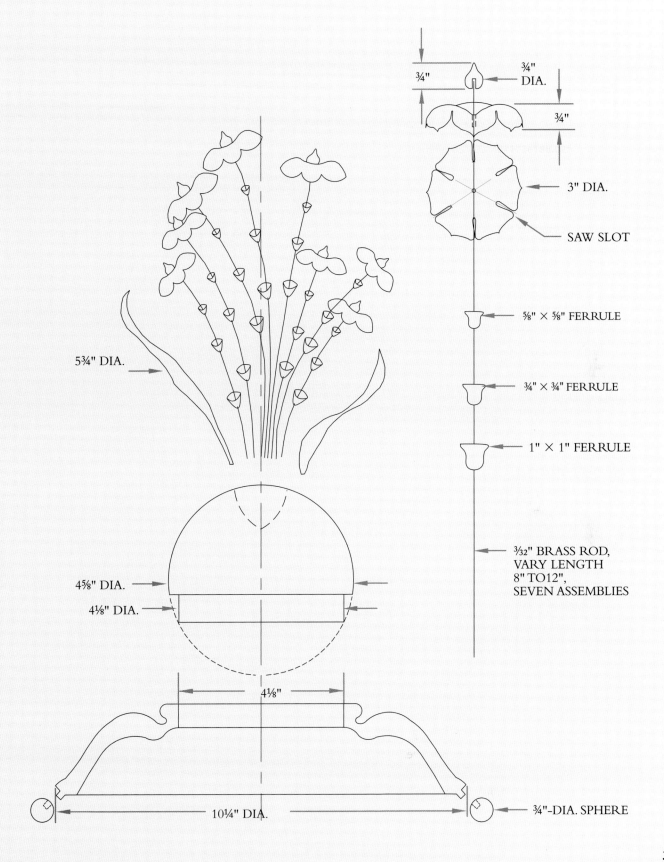

¾"
DIA.

¾"

¾"

3" DIA.

SAW SLOT

⅝" × ⅝" FERRULE

¾" × ¾" FERRULE

1" × 1" FERRULE

3/32" BRASS ROD,
VARY LENGTH
8" TO12",
SEVEN ASSEMBLIES

5¾" DIA.

4⅝" DIA.

4⅛" DIA.

4⅛"

10¼" DIA.

¾"-DIA. SPHERE

Making the Base

First turn the base of this project on a faceplate as you would the outside of a bowl. The 4⅛" ring and bead in which the sphere rests are turned ¾" deep. The rim of the turning is then turned to ¼" wide × ⅜" long. This rim will later be shaped to form the tenons upon which the four ¾" spheres are to be placed to make the feet for the project. The spheres are turned as detailed in Project Number 15 (see "Turning the Spheres," page 76, and the drawings on page 75).

The turning was then removed from the faceplate. A waste block on a 3" faceplate was turned to 4⅛" diameter with a flange of 5" diameter. This serves as a mandrel to reverse-chuck the base. Bring up the tailstock to support the turning for as long as possible. Sand and finish the part of the turning that will be used and then turn away the area under the tailstock live center (see "Sanding Suggestions" and "Finishes" earlier, on pages 8, 9, and 10).

Making the Body with an Opening

The sphere body was turned as detailed in Project Number 15, with one added procedure detailed below. Turn the sphere to about 4⅝" diameter.

With the sphere mounted between the cupped waste block and the tailstock, rotate the sphere to where the end grain is vertical or 90 degrees to the bed of the lathe. Measure 1¾" from the edge of the sphere on the tailstock side toward the center. Make a pencil mark around the sphere at that point. Turn a ledge to fit in the base 4⅛" in diameter (see the drawings).

Next, a wedge was carved away with mallet and chisel to create an opening in the top. Since the sphere is round and difficult to hold, place the sphere in a vise with soft jaws clamped on the flat part of the sphere that was turned to fit in the base. This will hold the carving securely. Pay attention to grain direction when laying out the area to be carved. Choose the area that will produce the best grain pattern. Side grain will carve easier and produce a better grain pattern to look as if the grain were opening to produce the burst of flowers. The area inside the opening was sanded with a rotary sanding drum in a reversible, high-speed mini-grinder that has a variable-speed control.

Turning the Flowers

1. To turn the flowers, a 3/32" hole was drilled in seven band-sawed ¾"-thick × 3"-diameter blanks.
2. A 3" diameter faceplate was attached to a waste block and turned down to an oval cone.
3. A ¾" length of 3/32" brass rod (available at local hobby shops) was drilled and glued in the center of the oval cone-shaped waste block (see the drawings). Double-stick carpet tape was applied to the contact area.
4. The outside of the flower was turned first, then sanded and finished.
5. With the brass rod acting to center and support the turning, the piece was reverse-chucked and then the underside of the flower was turned, sanded, and finished.

The flower centers were turned as described above with the same setup using the tailstock with a leather padded cup-type live center to hold the piece against the waste block and brass pin. The ferrules that are mounted on the brass rods were turned on the same waste block with the pin inserted. However, to get a better fit, the oval cone was reduced slightly in size and elongated. Blanks of ⅝" × ⅝", ¾" × ¾", and 1" × 1" were band-sawed and drilled. The double-stick tape was changed regularly. Light cuts are necessary to keep from overpowering the tape's capacity to hold.

THE FLOWERS—

In the photograph of the finished project, there are seven flower-and-stem sets mounted on varying lengths of 3/32" brass rod from 9" to 12" long.

The flowers and ferrules can be assembled on a length of brass rod and bent to various arcs. To mount these in the opening of the sphere, drill and arrange them two at a time. You will want to wait until all flower stems and leaves are arranged before the final gluing.

On the small-diameter pieces, a lathe speed of 2,000 rpm or more is preferred.

Carving and Shaping

❖ Once the turning process is completed, cover the base exterior with drafting tape and index to four sections.

❖ Lay out the area that is to be carved away. Check the graining on the piece to find the most desirable grain pattern. A band saw will speed up the carving process, but stay well away from lines.

Remember that the band saw cuts at 90 degrees to the table and the angle of the piece being cut can cause you to make a disastrous undercut.

❖ Shape by hand the ¼" tenons for the four spheres that will be the feet. Use a detail-carving knife to make the tenons. Since this area can be cross grain, drill and insert a ³⁄₃₂" × ¾" brass rod in the tenons for reinforcing before gluing on the spheres.

❖ To drill the spheres accurately, use a piece of waste scrap clamped to the drill-press table. Drill a ½" hole ⅜" deep.

This will serve as a cup to center the small spheres and make it easy to hold and drill. Drill the holes in the end grain of the spheres for better grain color and strength.

❖ Index the flowers after finishing, to six segments— 360 degrees divided by 6 equals 60 degrees. There is no need to cover them with tape. Make a pencil mark from the edge of rim toward the center ¾". You can band-saw away the pencil lines and detail the edge of the flower. Some hand sanding will be necessary.

Making the Leaves

Band-saw out the leaves to about ¹⁄₁₆" thick 6" to 10" long and varying from ¾" to 1¼" wide. Use the quarter-sawed edge as the surface of the leaves. This will give you more strength and flexibility and a better grain design. Use a belt sander with a fine grit to smooth away the saw marks. Hand sand with fine grits to a finish. Do not apply a finish or sealer to the leaves until after they are shaped by the following process. Make several sizes and lengths.

TWISTING & BENDING—

After you have sanded the leaves, soak them in a pan of water for about two hours. Remove each of them from the water individually and put them, one piece at a time, into the microwave oven for about 10 seconds on a high setting, similar to what I described for Project Number 4. This will take some experimentation as different woods respond to heat at different settings. You may need to turn the piece over and heat again. When the wood starts steaming or crackling, it is ready.

Wear a pair of protective leather gloves and remove the piece from the oven. S-l-o-w-l-y twist and bend until you have the desired shape. If the wood resists shaping, heat it a little more. Be careful not to get it too hot or the wood can discolor or, worse, catch on fire. Keep the water pan you took it out of close by!

When the piece is shaped to your satisfaction, while holding it in that shape with your gloves, run cold tap water over the piece—hands, gloves, and all. The wood will cool quickly and remain in that shape. This procedure is much the same as you would use to shape metal and may come to mind for other projects in the future.

After Bending

Lay the shaped pieces on a paper towel to dry and leave them overnight. They may then be hand sanded with the final grit before you apply the finish. Carefully drill holes along the opening of the sphere body using a long ³⁄₁₆" drill bit. Arrange the flowers in the holes. Use glue sparingly for this process.

When assembled and set with glue, the piece is then a compliment to the beautiful tree that gave the wood its first life.

7 TURNED WINE-BOTTLE STAND

I had made some cantilevered wine-bottle holders from dimensional lumber and was quite intrigued with the reaction of people to the seemingly precariously balanced bottle.

I decided to try using the same cantilever principle on pieces I turned on the lathe. To make this project work, you need to pay close attention to the dimensions.

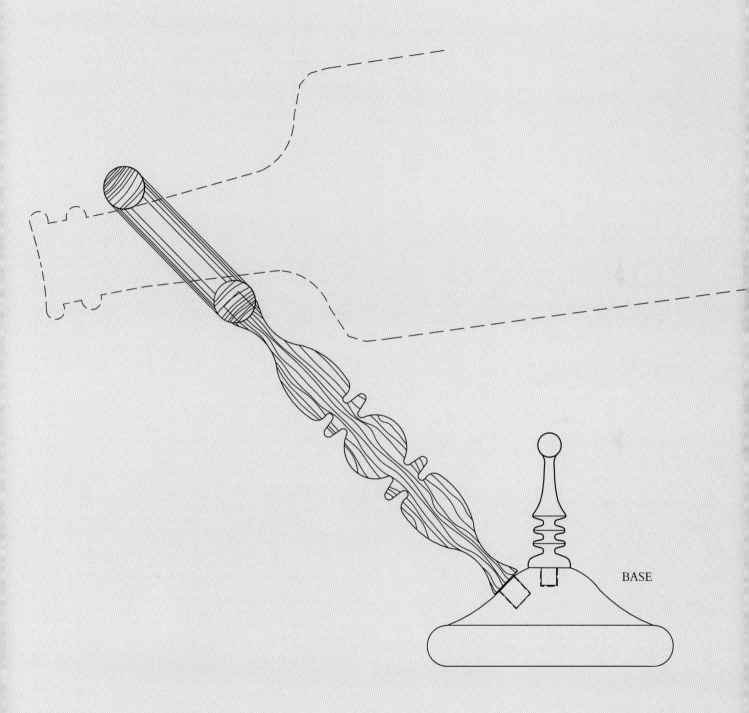

BASE

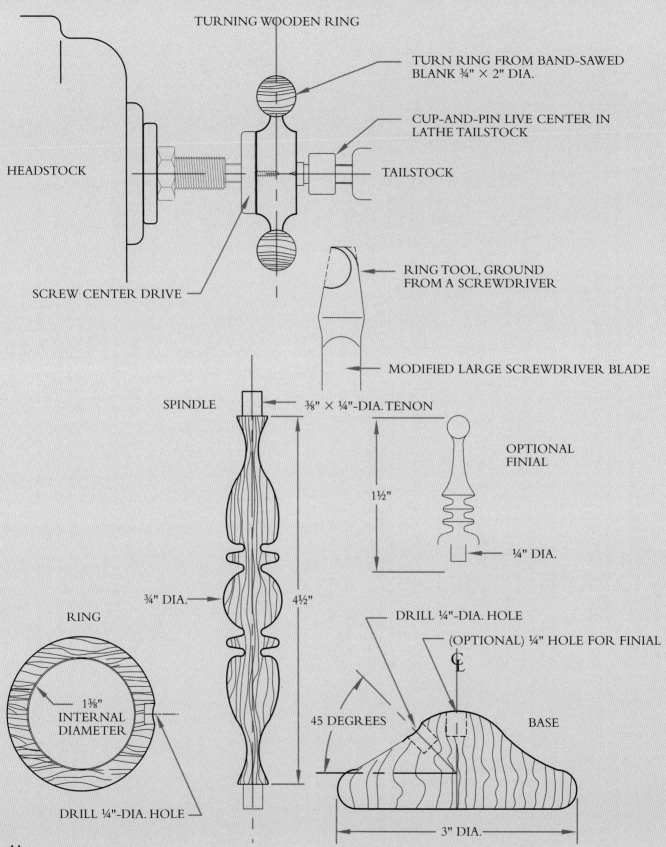

TURNING WOODEN RING

TURN RING FROM BAND-SAWED BLANK ¾" × 2" DIA.

CUP-AND-PIN LIVE CENTER IN LATHE TAILSTOCK

HEADSTOCK

TAILSTOCK

SCREW CENTER DRIVE

RING TOOL, GROUND FROM A SCREWDRIVER

MODIFIED LARGE SCREWDRIVER BLADE

SPINDLE

⅜" × ¼"-DIA. TENON

OPTIONAL FINIAL

1½"

¾" DIA.

4½"

¼" DIA.

RING

DRILL ¼"-DIA. HOLE

(OPTIONAL) ¼" HOLE FOR FINIAL

C̶L

1⅜" INTERNAL DIAMETER

45 DEGREES

BASE

DRILL ¼"-DIA. HOLE

3" DIA.

Turning the Ring

To turn the ring, a number of procedures are possible. I tried drilling a 1⅜" hole and using a wood mandrel, which requires dismounting and reversing. I used a screw chuck, which worked well and allowed access to both sides of the ring.

- ❖ But the easiest method is to band-saw the blank and mount it between a spur center and a live center. I used a ring tool I ground from a screw driver (as shown in the drawing). You can also use a ⅜" spindle gouge to shape the ring, and part off with a parting tool.
- ❖ After separation, use a 1"-diameter drum sander mounted in a drill chuck to smooth out the center.
- ❖ Drill a ¼" hole in the center of the edge of the ring on the end-grain side. A good way to position the bit is to add a skew line to the ring while it is still in the lathe.

Turning the Support Spindle

- ❖ Between centers turn the spindle into a ⅝"-to-¾" cylinder.
- ❖ Measure and mark the ends 4½" apart not including the tenon. Outside these lines, turn a ¼"-diameter × ⅜"-long tenon at each end.

The spindle turning gives you a chance to be creative and practice your skew techniques.

Turning the Base

- ❖ Turn the base about 3" in diameter with an area thick enough to drill a ¼" hole ⅜" deep at a 45-degree angle.

Again, you can be creative and free with the base, but the angle of the drilled hole is critical and needs to be accurate. On a couple, I added a finial to the base, just for looks. Align the grain and, with a square, make sure

DIMENSIONS—

The ring—the inside diameter of the ring—needs to be 1⅜". I made mine from mesquite and Texas ebony. Both of these woods have excellent lateral-grain strength. If your wood of choice has less strength, increase the thickness of the ring, but leave the inside diameter 1⅜".

Remember to keep the center of the hole the same distance from the center of the base. To do this, if you increase the thickness of the ring, deduct that same amount from the length of the spindle support turning.

Keep the basic dimensions for the spindle and the base, and the angle for the spindle, as close to the drawings as possible or the balance of the cantilever may be upset. But you can be creative with the turning details of the design, as I point out with each piece.

the ring is aligned so that an imaginary line through the center of the ring passes directly over the center of the stand. I use cyanoacrylate gap-filling glue. It sets quickly and holds well.

Finishing

I use Deft™ clear satin liquid with about 30 percent lacquer thinner added. This dries quicklya and seals the wood well, and a few coats give a nice finish. Let it set overnight and buff with a muslin wheel. (See "Sanding Suggestions" and "Finishes" earlier, on pages 8, 9, and 10.)

Before you drink the wine—enjoy turning!

8

TWIG-POT FUN

We all want to do a project that does not demand a lot of work, looks unique, and takes a minimum amount of time. Here is a twig-pot project that fulfills all of these requirements.

Selecting the Wood

As is always the case, the better the wood, the better the project results. I used mesquite for the contrasting color for the top and the foot. I used a scrap of maple from another project for the body. Select a piece for the body that is ¾" thick, 8" wide × 8" long. Make sure that the top piece is as thick as the body to which it will be glued. The foot should be a piece of waste, in this case mesquite, that is 1¼" thick × 2½" diameter.

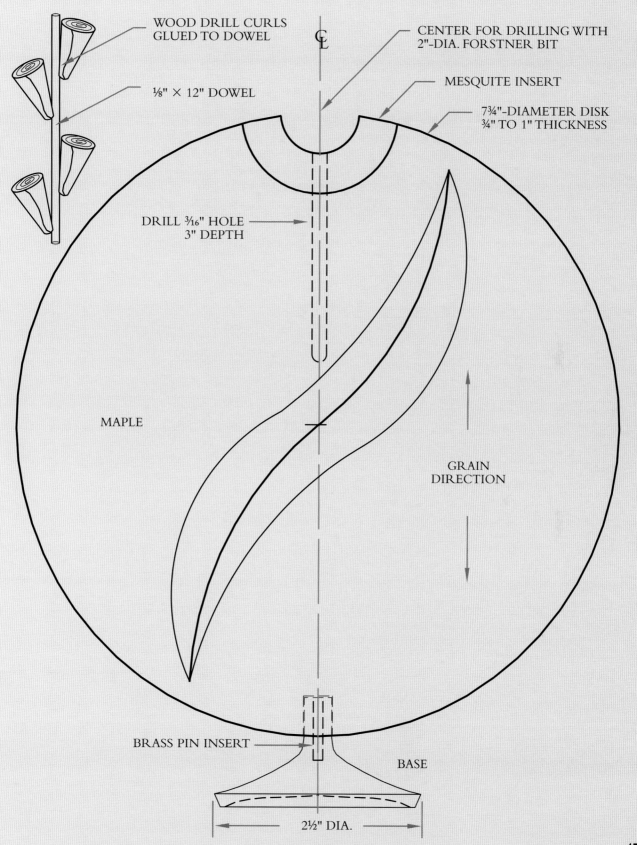

WOOD DRILL CURLS
GLUED TO DOWEL

⅛" × 12" DOWEL

C̶L̶

CENTER FOR DRILLING WITH
2"-DIA. FORSTNER BIT

MESQUITE INSERT

7¾"-DIAMETER DISK
¾" TO 1" THICKNESS

DRILL ³⁄₁₆" HOLE
3" DEPTH

MAPLE

GRAIN
DIRECTION

BRASS PIN INSERT

BASE

2½" DIA.

Making the Body

With a compass, draw a circle as large as the wood will allow. With a straightedge draw a line with the grain from edge to edge using the center of the circle marked by the compass. Mark each edge of the body of the piece as this will become the top and bottom of the project.

❖ On one edge, drill a ⅜" hole ½" deep. This will be for the foot. This is easily done before turning using either a horizontal drill press or drill press with a vertical centering vise.

❖ On the opposite edge, with the board flat, using a 2" Forstner bit, clamp the piece securely to the drill table with a waste scrap underneath.

Place the center point of the drill at the edge of the board on the marked line. With medium pressure drill through the piece, creating a half hole for gluing the insert.

SAVE THE SHAVINGS—

Before you do anything else, note the shavings made while drilling with the Forstner bit. They should come off of the drill as curly cones. Carefully gather these.

Glue the shavings with C/A glue to a ¹⁄₁₆" dowel 8" to 10" long to become flowerlike twigs for the pot from which they came.

Turning the Top Insert

❖ Turn a 2"-diameter insert using double-stick carpet tape on a waste block held tightly with the live center. You only need turn the diameter to fit the drilled hole. The surfaces will be shaped with the other piece after gluing.

❖ Glue in the insert with C/A glue, and with a 1" Forstner bit, drill as before to create a gap in the top.

❖ Use a Forstner bit that cuts a smooth hole, so very little sanding will be required later.

❖ Using double-stick carpet tape on a waste block about 2" in diameter, center the 8"-diameter piece and secure it in place with the tailstock.

Place two layers of heavy leather on the live cup center to prevent marking the finished surface of the body. You will be able to turn and sand both sides with this setup except under the tape on one side and the leather on the other. The little bit of hand sanding is easier than trying to recenter after turning one side with a different procedure.

Embellishing the Surface

You can be creative in your surface embellishment and carry it around the edge to tie in with the same design on the opposite side. Use your imagination.

❖ Place drafting tape over the sides and draw a design (such as an elongated "S" in this example) and sand away one side of the line to about 1" width × ¼" depth on the front side.

❖ Use a 2" sanding disk mounted in the lathe chuck and work the piece against the spinning disk to do the sanding.

Start with about 120-grit and proceed through 320-grit. This will create a light-and-shadow effect.

Turning and Adding the Foot

❖ Glue on a 1¼"-thick × 2½"-diameter band-sawed blank and turn the base. As always, turn the large diameters first, secured with the live center, before you turn the small ⅜" × ½" tenon.

Note: In some woods the grain of the tenon may be a weak point. If this is the case, drill and insert a ⅛" brass pin of appropriate length. It will be hidden and will strengthen the tenon.

❖ Install the foot and drill the hole for the twigs.

❖ The foot glued in place will allow you to stand the piece vertically on the drill press.

❖ Drill a ⅜"-diameter hole 3" deep straight down into the insert.

Finishing

See "Sanding Suggestions" and "Finishes" earlier, on pages 8, 9, and 10.

Twig pots are fun to make. With the curly flowers, you can show off how much you enjoy turning!

9

SCRAP WOOD MUSIC BOX

This project is the result of my determination to make a turning from a particularly nice piece of mesquite that was ¾" thick × 5" wide × 10" long. I added an electronic, light-activated music box inside the lid to create a surprise for anyone who opened the box.

Setting Up for Turning

The board had been planed and was smooth on both sides, allowing a good bond with double-stick tape on a waste block. Use a small (3") faceplate and attach a waste block of the same diameter that is about 3" or 4" long. Taper the end of the block away from the screws down to about 2". Use 2"-wide tape that has fiberglass reinforcing.

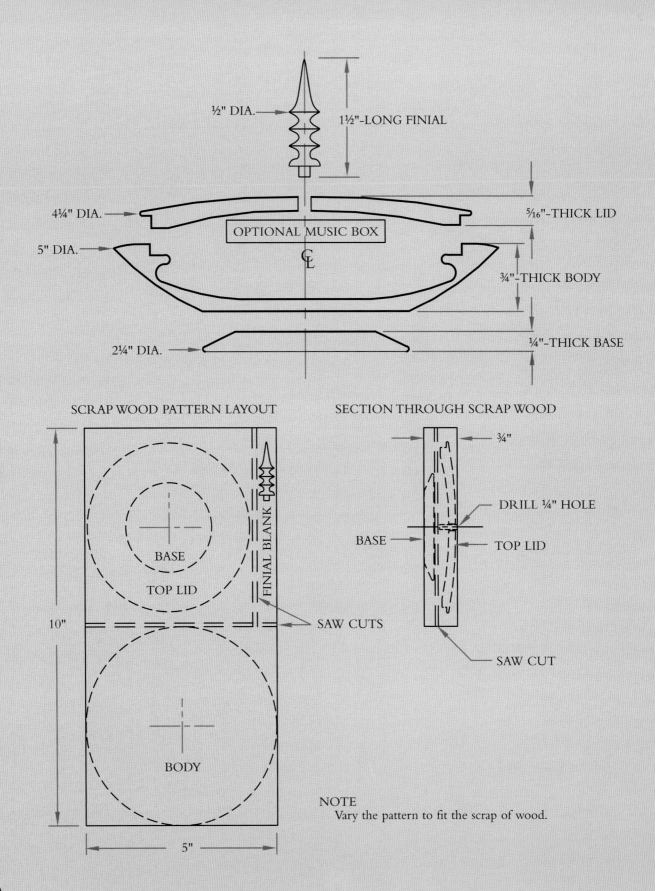

½" DIA.

1½"-LONG FINIAL

4¼" DIA.

OPTIONAL MUSIC BOX

C̶L

5/16"-THICK LID

5" DIA.

¾"-THICK BODY

2¼" DIA.

¼"-THICK BASE

SCRAP WOOD PATTERN LAYOUT

SECTION THROUGH SCRAP WOOD

¾"

BASE

TOP LID

BASE

TOP LID

DRILL ¼" HOLE

FINIAL BLANK

SAW CUTS

SAW CUT

10"

BODY

5"

NOTE
Vary the pattern to fit the scrap of wood.

Preparing Blanks

1. Scribe with a compass the largest circle possible on one end of the board. This will be the body of the box.
2. Choose the area with the best graining and color to become the lid. The base, top, and finial will come from the remaining half. (See the drawing.)
3. Remove the blank for the finial, then re-saw the remaining piece into blanks for the top and base. Divide the piece with a centerline down the edge of the board. Use a guide to keep it vertical on the band-saw table and saw it into two halves. For safety, re-saw before you band-saw it round.
4. Band-saw the body round.

Turning the Pieces

5. Place the pin of a cup and pin live center on the compass point. This will center the turning against the double-stick tape placed on the waste block.
6. Using the tailstock, press the blank against the tape. Turn the blank to a balanced cylinder and remove the tailstock.
7. Make the shallow mortise groove for the lid to fit with a parting tool. Shape the box and hollow. Do not sand the area where the lid will fit. Finish and remove from the tape.
8. The base is turned using the above procedure and the same waste block. Remove the old double-stick tape from the waste block and replace with fresh tape. Turn and finish the base.

Remember to create a concave area in the bottom of the base so that the piece will sit steadily on a tabletop or other flat surface.

9. For turning the lid, drill a ¼" hole in the blank. Use a drill press so that the hole will be straight. Also, drill a ¼" hole ½" deep in the center of the waste block using a tailstock mounted Jacobs chuck.
10. Glue a ¾" length of ¼" birch dowel into the waste block. This will serve to center the lid.
11. Apply new double-stick tape around the dowel and place the outside of the top against the tape. Use the tailstock live center to create pressure against the tape.
12. Measure, mark, and turn the inside of the box lid.

Use the body to check the fit of the lid if there is concern. With this setup you can remove the tailstock and have access to check the lid fit. Sand and finish the inside of the lid.

Remove and reverse the lid on the waste block using new tape. You may want to shape the surface of the waste block to fit the curvature of the inside of the lid before applying the new tape. It may not be necessary, but for good practice, place a double layer of leather between the cup-and-pin live center and the lid so the surface will not be marked. Press the turning against the tape with the tailstock while you start the turning. After the basic shape has been turned, the tailstock can be removed and the tape will hold.

Turn the finial using a small ⅜" spur center and cup type live center. Using the parting tool and calipers, turn a ¼" diameter tenon the same length as the depth of the hole in the lid. The sharp beads and coves are turned using a ½" skew. Sand and finish the finial.

Glue the finial in the lid using C/A glue. Using a small amount of glue, center and glue the base to the body, paying attention to grain direction.

ADDING A MUSIC BOX—

A battery-powered electronic music box makes a nice addition to the lidded box. Use a small amount of double-stick tape to secure it to the inside of the lid. Such music boxes are available from various suppliers including Klockit, P. O. Box 636, Lake Geneva WI 53147, 1-800-556-2548, www.klockit.com, email: klockit@klock it.com.

Now, you get the bonus of admiration and surprise when the box is inspected.

Finishing

See "Sanding Suggestions" and "Finishes" earlier, on pages 8, 9, and 10. This is a wonderful project for giving new life to a scrap of well-figured wood.

10   MUSIC BOX BALLET

The beauty of a graceful ballerina moving to music inspired this project, but the centerpiece can be anything you wish: a clown figure, square-dancers, a turned bouquet of flowers, or how about a special turning? In fact, you do not have to make the support arms or the hanging figure; you can utilize the plans of the base only as a musical rotating display.

Because it carves easily, turns well, and presents a beautiful grain pattern when finished, I selected butternut as the material for this project.

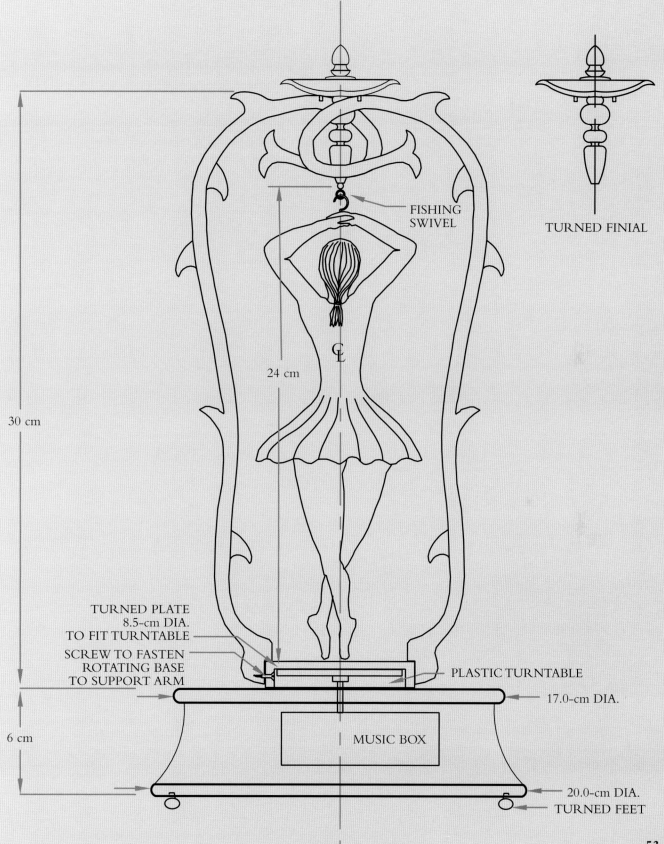

FISHING
SWIVEL

TURNED FINIAL

24 cm

30 cm

TURNED PLATE
8.5-cm DIA.
TO FIT TURNTABLE

SCREW TO FASTEN
ROTATING BASE
TO SUPPORT ARM

PLASTIC TURNTABLE

17.0-cm DIA.

6 cm

MUSIC BOX

20.0-cm DIA.
TURNED FEET

53

Turning the Base

❖ To turn the base, drill a ¼" hole in the center of a band-sawed blank 8" in diameter × 2" to 2¼" thick. For any project that will eventually have a hole drilled in the center, I generally drill the hole first and use it as a lathe-mounting method.

USING A THREADED-ROD CENTER—

If you remove the screw from a screw center that has a Morse taper for headstock mounting, you will generally find that it is threaded with a National Course standard thread. If it is not threaded inside and are held by a set screw, it is not difficult to tap to fit a standard thread.

❖ You can then screw in a piece of threaded rod cut to proper length, insert it through the turning blank, and tighten the piece down with a flat washer and jam-nut. Add an acorn nut to the end of the threaded rod.

❖ You can then bring up the tailstock with a cup center to engage the acorn nut, allowing you to turn one side, remove and reverse the turning, and still be centered.

Note: The hole in the blank should be drilled on a drill press so that the blank will be parallel with the axis of the lathe and at 90 degrees to the mounting surface. Obviously, there are several other options that you might use for turning this piece, including a regular screw chuck, but this method is certainly worth a try.

❖ You can use any regular bowl gouge; I like the super-flute gouges for control. Leave a flange on the base for installing the feet. Index to 120 degrees to drill holes for mounting three turned feet. Three balance points (feet) make the piece sit steadily.

❖ All three feet can be turned at the same time using a small ⅜" spur center and a cup center. The lengths of the feet should be identical. Cut off the feet with a saw and belt-sand the tenons to length. (See drawing in Project Number 18.)

The music box should be mounted underneath the base with a strap of ⅜" wide thin brass formed into a "U" bracket and held in place with screws. Before securing the retainer strap, fit the turntable to the music box and make sure that it does not bind against the sides of the drilled hole. Even a small amount of friction can stall the tiny motor that drives the music box.

The rotating base is made to cover the plastic turntable much as you would make a box lid or jar lid. I used a faceplate with a waste block that had been turned flat on the front. Double-stick carpet tape will hold nicely on a band-sawed blank. Use the tailstock and a live center to hold the blank in place as long as you can. Then back the live center off and turn away the peg that remains. There is no need to sand the underside because the plastic turntable will fit inside and cover this surface.

Support Arms, Figure & Finial

These should be from the same piece of wood to maximize the grain match. The support arms are drawn from a pattern with the grain running up the arms for strength. The finial will add strength and stability to the arms when assembled. Short pieces of birch dowel glued in place fix the finial to the support arms. A ³⁄₁₆" hole drilled in the lower end of the finial will accept a small fishing swivel—get the stainless-steel ball-bearing type that turns freely and will not rust.

For the centerpiece I carved a ballerina. This figure has a relatively high degree of difficulty, but is interesting to carve. Pay special attention to sanding and finishing techniques to achieve a match in wood colors and grain patterns.

To strengthen the area where the hands meet and the grain is weak across the hands, soak the area with thin C/A glue before finishing. This will lessen the possibility of breakage.

11

BIRD-WATCHERS' CAROUSEL MUSIC BOX

The theme for this project was selected because my wife and I enjoy rather serious recreational bird-watching. With my interest in trees and shrubs and hers in butterflies and flowers, it was natural to study the other colorful inhabitants of our incredibly beautiful countryside.

Turning the Base

The base was turned using the same method as in Project Number 10. You can, however, turn the base using the normal procedure for turning a bowl. The piece would then be drilled when finished. Leave an area to drill and insert the turned feet in the edge of the base. Index the feet at 120 degrees so it will sit steadily on a flat surface.

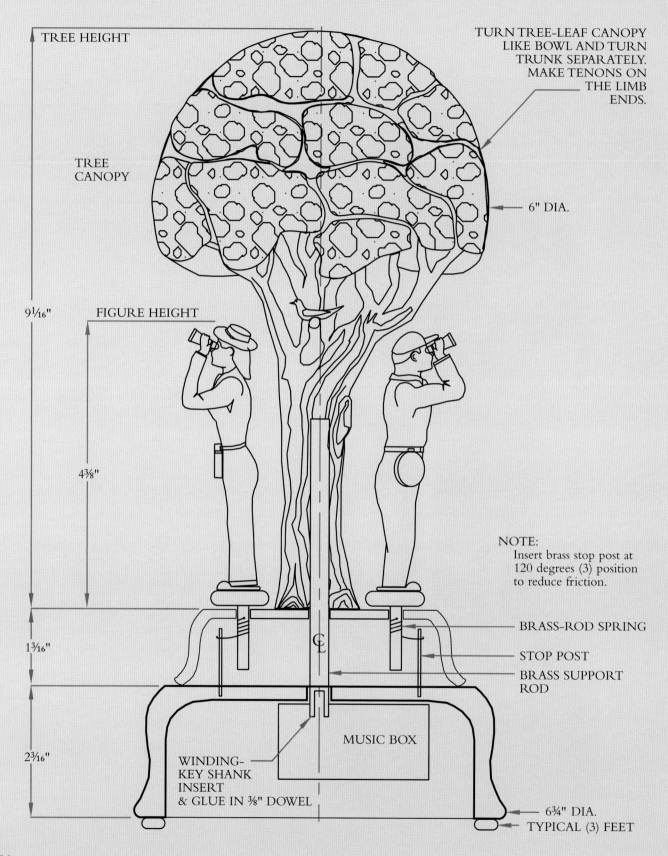

TREE HEIGHT

TURN TREE-LEAF CANOPY
LIKE BOWL AND TURN
TRUNK SEPARATELY.
MAKE TENONS ON
THE LIMB
ENDS.

TREE
CANOPY

6" DIA.

9¹⁄₁₆"

FIGURE HEIGHT

4³⁄₈"

NOTE:
Insert brass stop post at
120 degrees (3) position
to reduce friction.

C̶L̶

BRASS-ROD SPRING

1³⁄₁₆"

STOP POST

BRASS SUPPORT
ROD

MUSIC BOX

2³⁄₁₆"

WINDING-
KEY SHANK
INSERT
& GLUE IN ³⁄₈" DOWEL

6³⁄₄" DIA.

TYPICAL (3) FEET

56

Attaching the Music Box

Mount the music box underneath using a ⅜"-wide strap of brass (as in Project Number 10) bent into a bracket with a pair of pliers. Leave enough thickness—about ⅜"—in the top of the base so that the screws do not go through. This also acts as a guide for the rotating superstructure.

Unlike bowls, where thinness is an indication of skill, music boxes require thicker walls to act both as guides and sound-transfer agents.

Turning the Platform

In making the rotating platform, you will use the same procedure as you did for the base—following the method in Project No. 10 or using the normal procedure for turning a bowl. Again, leave the material about ⅜" thick to act as a guide for the superstructure.

Indexing

When you index at 120 degrees for the feet, you can also index for the three stop posts on a 3⅞" circle. These stop posts will be made of ⅛" brass rod 1" long.

Making the Springs

The brass springs that give action to the figures are made from 0.015"-diameter wire. Most hobby shops carry a display assortment of various-diameter brass rods 12" long. One 12" section of this small-diameter rod will be enough to make both springs.

Use a pin drill and a ½"-long piece of the brass rod (used as the bit) to drill a hole in the figure-support dowel to anchor the spring. By hand, wrap the rod around the support dowel until you have about three coils with approximately 1" extending straight out to the side. This extension should be long enough to engage the stop posts as it rotates. The greater the length, the further the figures will rotate—and the more power it will take. This may take a few adjustments before it works.

The Figures

The figures in the example are bird-watchers carved from basswood. Other suggestions for figures are a

HOW IT ROTATES—

In this project, as in others, the energy of the winding key on a fully wound music box is utilized to create music and movement with a surprising twist. The mechanism is wound by rotating the tree canopy clockwise until fully wound. As the tree and figures move in the unwinding process, the music starts to play.

The figures are mounted on a dowel to which a spring is attached under the rotating base. The free end of the spring is extended so that it contacts three brass posts placed at 120 degrees. This causes the figures to slowly rotate a few degrees until the spring passes the post. The surprise in people's faces when the figures snap back is more than worth the extra effort.

Three posts instead of two or four was decided by trial and error. In the first prototype type, it was discovered that with the two carved figures (an even number) and two or four posts (also even numbers) the music mechanism did not have enough power to compress both springs that operate the figures at the same time. Therefore, it is important to use an even number of figures and an odd number of posts. This configuration will eliminate the possibility of two spring's being compressed at the same time and still give the desired amount of action to the figures.

golfer putting a ball, a fly-fisherman casting a fly, a tennis player stroking a ball, or use your creative imagination to develop your own project.

In carving these figures, draw to scale a front and side profile of the subject. It helps to include in your drawing all of the details to be carved later. Put in a centerline to keep each figure symmetrical.

TRANSFERRING IMAGES—

A hot iron will transfer a freshly made photocopy from paper to the wood. Graphite paper from the hobby shop will also work and is available in colors. If the wood is dark, use white graphite paper. Carbon paper leaves a residue on the wood that, in some cases, is undesirable.

Use a medium No. 2 pencil to draw on the figure as you carve. The most often, used tool in your carving box should be a sharp pencil. Using basswood for the figures makes the carving process fairly easy. You may however, wish to use the same wood on the entire project for color, compatibility, and aesthetic considerations.

Upon completion of the carved figures, carefully drill a hole in their bases to accept the figure support dowels. Usually a ¾"-deep hole in the base is ample and a ¼" or ⁵⁄₁₆" birch dowel works nicely for the support. Insert the dowel in the prepared hole in the rotating base. The spring is then installed by inverting the assembly and working in what will be the underside. Make sure the figures do not bind against the sides of the drilled holes.

A birch dowel ⅜" diameter × 5" long will serve as the support for the tree and as a winding stem for the music box. The winding shaft of the music box is threaded to accept the winding key. To attach the support dowel to the threaded music-box shaft, grind off the ears of the winding key and glue the round key shaft into a hole drilled in the bottom of the dowel. This will allow you to assemble and disassemble the project as needed.

Turning & Carving the Tree

The tree is a challenge both to turn and to carve. First, turn the trunk and limbs in one piece. Make a template of the branch arc from lightweight cardboard. This will serve as a guide for making the inside of the canopy.

The limbs come from the trunk in all directions so you can be as free in the design as you wish as you lay them out for carving. Note that they are larger at the trunk and get smaller in diameter as they reach up to the canopy. Carve a small tenon on the end of at least three of the limbs so that you can affix the canopy to the trunk by drilling matching holes to fit.

Turning & Carving the Canopy

The canopy is turned as you would an open bowl. Use the template of the arc of the branches to shape the inside of the canopy. This is necessary in that the limbs go in different directions and must all intersect the canopy at the same time to fit.

To carve the canopy, notice that in live trees clusters of leaves appear at the ends of branches and limbs. Design your canopy to have open areas and clusters of leaves at the ends of the limbs. The open areas add reality to the carving so that you can see through to the limbs. Use a small ⅛" Vee gouge to create both bark texture and leaf texture. Bark is made with ¾"- to 1"-long sweeps of the Vee gouge—not in a straight line. Curve each cut slightly one way or another. If you create a knot in the trunk, curve the bark around it as the tree would naturally grow. Bark grooves get shorter and smaller as the limbs reduce in size.

Make the leaves with small random diamond patterns. It is always a good idea to do a sample on a scrap of the same wood to see how it looks before you carve the actual piece. Make the clusters of leaves so that the upper clusters slightly overlap the ones below as if they were shingles on a house. This will add to the realism and it is the way trees grow. Use a slight undercut on the lower edge of the clusters.

Finishing

See "Sanding Suggestions" and "Finishes" earlier, on pages 8, 9, and 10. As you assemble the finished pieces, take care not to screw the trunk down tight against the rotating base. It is best not to glue the support dowel into the trunk until you have made this adjustment.

Once the project is complete, you should have a brass plate made with the title of the piece and your name.

12

FLYING-SAUCER MUSIC BOX

The wheels roll, the propeller turns, and the music box plays in this most beguiling project. It requires discipline and skill but provides challenge and reward. It contains procedures that can be used in many other projects. The use of different chucking systems to produce the twelve turnings and two carvings will bring together this amusing, musical flying saucer.

Selecting the Wood
As in every project, the fun starts with searching for a suitable piece of wood. The wood in this example was a long-stored piece of "monkey pod" from Hawaii given to me by my friend, the internationally acclaimed woodturner Ron Kent.

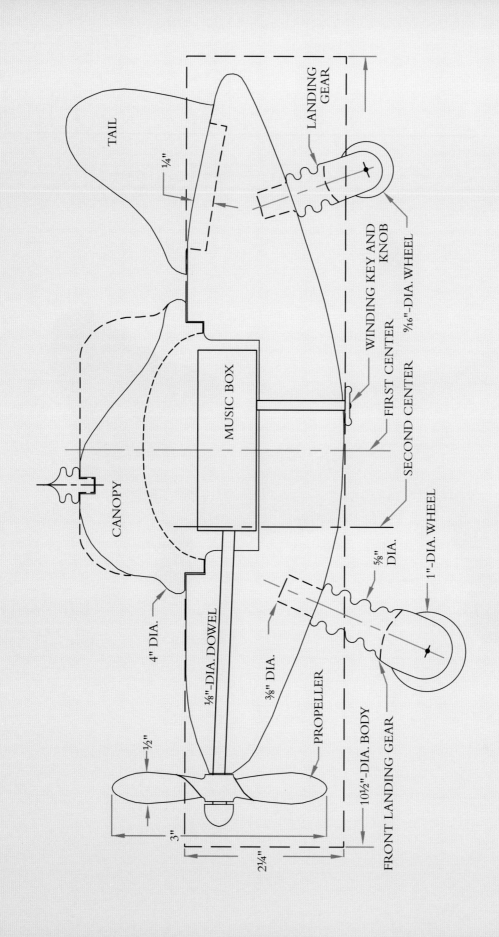

TAIL

¼"

LANDING
GEAR

WINDING KEY AND
KNOB

FIRST CENTER

%6"-DIA. WHEEL

SECOND CENTER

MUSIC BOX

CANOPY

4" DIA.

⅛"-DIA. DOWEL

⅜" DIA.

⅝"
DIA.

1"-DIA. WHEEL

½"

PROPELLER

10½"-DIA. BODY

FRONT LANDING GEAR

3"

2¼"

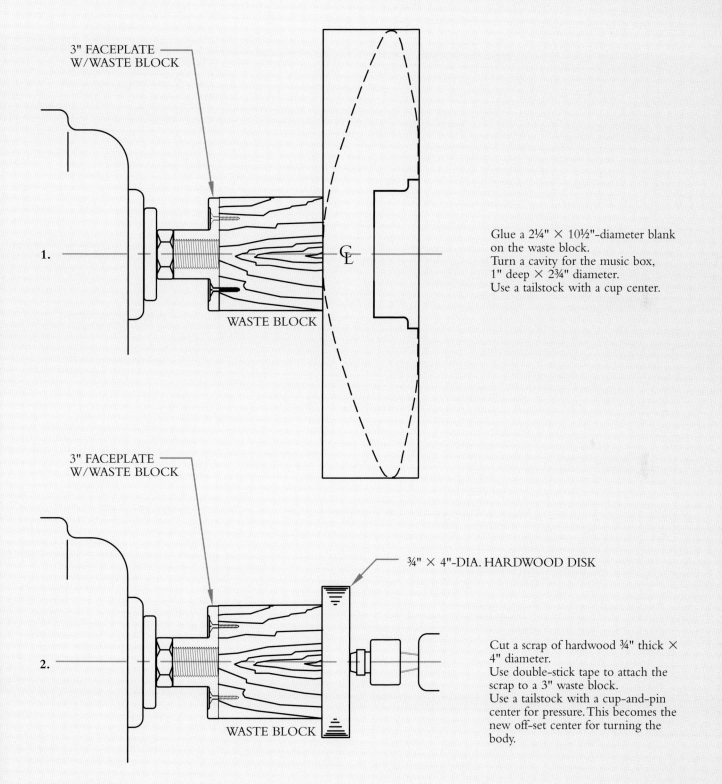

3" FACEPLATE
W/WASTE BLOCK

WASTE BLOCK

1.

C
L

Glue a 2¼" × 10½"-diameter blank
on the waste block.
Turn a cavity for the music box,
1" deep × 2¾" diameter.
Use a tailstock with a cup center.

3" FACEPLATE
W/WASTE BLOCK

¾" × 4"-DIA. HARDWOOD DISK

WASTE BLOCK

2.

Cut a scrap of hardwood ¾" thick ×
4" diameter.
Use double-stick tape to attach the
scrap to a 3" waste block.
Use a tailstock with a cup-and-pin
center for pressure. This becomes the
new off-set center for turning the
body.

61

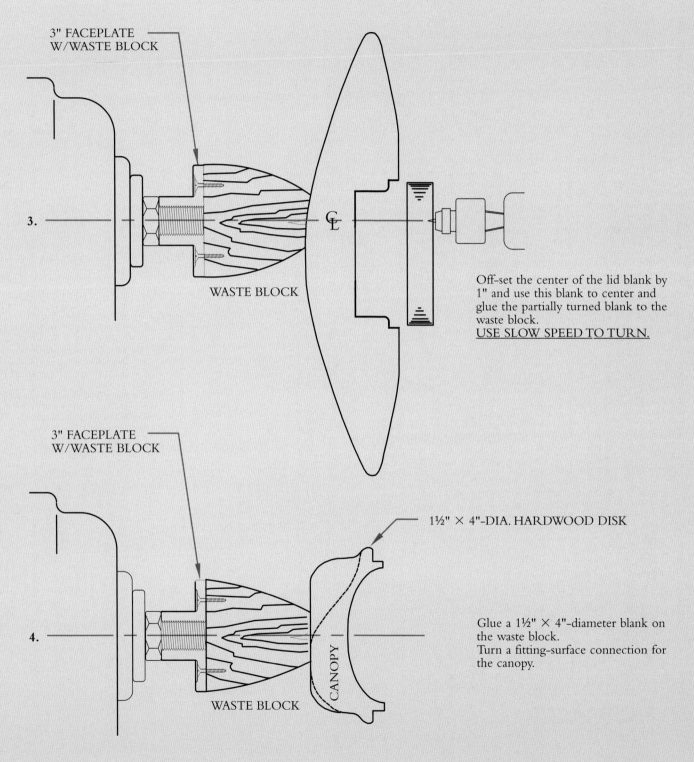

3" FACEPLATE
W/WASTE BLOCK

3.

WASTE BLOCK

$\mathrm{C\!\!\!\!\!L}$

Off-set the center of the lid blank by
1" and use this blank to center and
glue the partially turned blank to the
waste block.
<u>USE SLOW SPEED TO TURN.</u>

3" FACEPLATE
W/WASTE BLOCK

4.

WASTE BLOCK

CANOPY

1½" × 4"-DIA. HARDWOOD DISK

Glue a 1½" × 4"-diameter blank on
the waste block.
Turn a fitting-surface connection for
the canopy.

The darkness of the wood was a consideration for the body of the project. A contrasting light-colored wood from the basswood pile would do nicely for the canopy and propeller. Scraps from the band-sawed body would work for the tail, wheels, and landing gear. Now all that is necessary is to get them into the right shape. It is amazing how once you have the idea, plan, and wood you feel that the project is half complete!

Turning the Pieces

1. Using a 3" faceplate with a waste block, attach the band-sawed 10½" × 2¼" blank with C/A glue.

Bring up the tailstock with a cup-and-pin live center to hold the blank against the waste block. Use of the tailstock is always a good safety procedure.

2. Turn the body to a balanced cylinder and slightly round off the front and back of the piece (see the drawings).

3. With the turning balanced, it is time to remove the tailstock and turn the cavity that will hold the music box. The cavity should be 1" deep and 2¾" diameter. This can be done with a Forstner bit, but a large bit creates a lot of torque on the glue joint. It is best to drill a smaller ½" hole to the proper depth and excavate with a bowl gouge.

4. Turn a mortise shoulder to accommodate the next procedure and later the canopy-styled lid. This mortise should be about ¼" wide and ¼" deep.

Remove the body from the waste block. Usually a rap with a mallet from the back side will break the glue seal. If not, run the tailstock up, seating the live center in the bottom of the music box cavity, and, with a parting tool, reduce the size of the glue joint on the waste block side to about 1". Then with the lathe turned off and the tailstock retracted, it will come loose with a bump from the heel of your hand.

Dress the face of the waste block to remove the glue and have a clean, flat surface. Band-saw out a piece of scrap hardwood ¾" thick by 4" in diameter. Use double-stick carpet tape to attach the turning to the waste block. You can run up the tailstock to create pressure against the tape.

5. Turn the piece to fit the mortise shoulder in the music-box cavity. This piece will serve as a tailstock chuck to enable you to do the off-set turning in the next procedure.

The center mark made by the tailstock in the turned ¾"-thick piece will serve as a reference point. From this point, measure 1" to the side and establish a new center by indenting the live center. This will now become the new off-set center for turning the body.

Clean the waste block surface and—using the new off-set center—glue the bottom of the body to the waste block. The block inserted in the canopy cavity held in place with the new tailstock center will secure the piece to turn away the edges that will form the saucer shape. The main purpose of this procedure is to have the canopy off-center toward the propeller and have room to install the carved tail in the top of the turned surface.

TURNING SAFELY—

No one ever plans to go to the shop to have an accident. When you read or hear comments on safety, remember that it is your personal safety to which they refer.

It is important for safety to turn the lathe on at a slow speed to do this part of the project. If you have the luxury of variable speed control, bring the speed up slowly until you have the project in near balance. If you have step pulleys, use the slowest speed available. Never stand directly in line with the unbalanced turning. Standing to the side will prevent accidents or injuries if the piece should come out of the lathe.

6. With your favorite spindle gouge, turn the top so that it is slightly oval. On the bottom, work from the waste block to the edge, leaving the edge rounded and about ½" thick.

For this part of the project, it is easier to do the sanding after the piece is removed from the lathe. A random orbital sander works quickly and allows you to blend the area that was attached to the waste block into the shape of the rest of the turning.

7. Turn the waste block down to 2" diameter outside the screws and attach a band-sawed 4"-diameter × 1½"-thick piece of basswood with C/A glue. This will become the canopy and is made like a box lid.

LINING THINGS UP—

Once the canopy is finished, it is time to establish a centerline to line up the center for the hole for the propeller, the center of the music-box cavity, and the slot to be carved out for the tail. A strip of drafting tape either side of the cavity will allow pencil lines to be drawn. Mark the centerline for the tail piece and a point for the hole to be drilled for the propeller shaft.

The propeller shaft is made of a length of ⅛" birch dowel about 3½" long. The shaft will press-fit into the center of the rotating drum of a Sankyo 18-note music box (available from Klockit, see page 51). Effectively, this utilizes the music mechanism as a right-angle gear box. The winding stem will extend through the bottom of the cavity to be wound underneath the saucer while the propeller shaft extends through the edge of the piece to turn the propeller.

The real thought-provoking and perplexing problem comes with establishing the centerline (see heading at right) when positioning the body to drill a ⅛" hole from the centered edge of the turning to exactly hit the center of a ⅛" hole in the end of the rotating drum of the music box.

8. Using calipers, make the lip to fit the opening for the music box. If you do not trust the calipers, turn off the lathe and try the fit by holding the base up to the canopy. This is only one of the benefits of turning the inside of the box lid first.

9. Sand and finish the inside of the lid. Do not sand on the fitted surface.

10. Turn the edge of the top of the lid and slightly taper the top toward the waste block. This is all of the shaping that can be done on the lathe. Remove the turning from the waste block.

Sanding to Shape

Refer to the drawings for the shape. A belt sander with an aggressive grit will work quickly to sand the soft basswood into shape. Be careful not to sand away the flange made to hide the lid connection. By sanding away one side, the illusion of being turned off center is created as well as being similar to the shape of an airplane canopy. Although it requires some hand sanding to finish, the area worked is small and finishes quickly.

Establishing the Centerline

❖ With the lid off of the cavity and the music mechanism placed inside but unattached, put a ⅛" dowel 8" long in the drill chuck of a horizontal drill press.

❖ Fill a medium-sized plastic bag about one third full of shavings. Make a nest in the shavings bag for the body of the saucer until it sets steady.

❖ Extend the dowel in the chuck out over the turning.

❖ Adjust the pitch of the body until the center of the edge and the center of the hole in the rotating drum are equal distance from the center of the dowel. Measure and note this distance.

❖ Remove the dowel from the chuck and install a ⅛" drill bit.

❖ Raise the table the noted measurement and drill the hole. The bit will come out into the cavity and line up with the hole in the drum.

Let the drill bit run a moment in the drilled hole to burnish the inside of the hole. This will minimize friction when the propeller shaft turns. If the hole is slightly off, adjust the position of the music mechanism with a cardboard shim.

- With the shaft in place in the drum, anchor the mechanism after you have drilled the ³⁄₁₆" hole out of the bottom for the winding key. The propeller shaft should extend out from the edge about ¾" to mount the propeller and finial hub.

Propeller, Tail & Landing Gear

Carve a propeller ½" wide and 3" long. Drill a ⅛" hole in the center of the blank before carving. This will serve to mount on the shaft when finished and helps keep the carving symmetrical. The shaft will turn clockwise facing the propeller hub.

- For the tail, cut a pattern out of ½"-thick scrap with the grain running vertically. Carve a tenon on one end, ¼" × ¼" × 1¼" long, to fit into a slot carved through the tape into the back (see drawing).
- A belt sander makes quick and easy work of shaping the tail piece. A penciled centerline on the stock will help keep the tail symmetrical. Leave enough wood to hand sand the piece with finer grits for a good polished finish.

Before installing the tail, turn the body over and match the centerline on the top with another piece of tape on the bottom.

- On the bottom from the edge of the body on the tail side measure 1¾" down the centerline and mark a point for a hole for the tail wheel.
- From the propeller side, measure 2½" down the centerline and draw a line perpendicular at this point.
- Measure 1½" along each direction away from the centerline at 90 degrees for the drill hole point to accept the two front landing gears.
- Drill holes for the landing gear ⅜" diameter × ½" deep at 90 degrees to the surface. Because the area to which the gear will be attached is oval, the wheels will naturally set splayed and look correct. This drilling is best done by hand to keep from building an angle jig or using time to set up the drill press.
- To turn the landing gear, use a four-jaw chuck. Turn a ⅜" tenon ½" long on one end to insert into the drilled hole.
- For the two front landing gears, turn a cylinder ⅝" diameter × 1" long and a cylinder ¾" diameter × 1" long on the end opposite the ⅜" tenon. In the ⅝"-

diameter area turn a series of four sharp beads and coves using a ½" skew.
- Sand and finish while on the lathe. See "Sanding Suggestions" and "Finishing" earlier, on pages 8, 9, and 10. The ¾" cylinder will be where the wheel will fit.

With it removed from the lathe, scroll-saw a slot in the ¾" end ⅜" wide × ¾" deep, centered, for mounting the wheels. Cut the slot with the grain to prevent splitting the wood when the weight is on the wheels.

Turning the Wheels

- To turn the wheels, scroll-saw out two blanks ⁵⁄₁₆" thick × 1" in diameter. Using the compass center-point mark as a reference, drill a ¹⁄₁₆" hole.
- Set a Jacobs chuck in the headstock and using a short length of ⁹⁄₁₆" brass rod, mount the blank on the rod.

A live center point will provide the friction to both center and turn the wheel when pressed into the hole opposite the brass rod. This setup will allow reversing and access to both sides of the wheel. Sand and finish while it is on the lathe.

- To turn the rear landing gear, use the same system. The tenon is ⅜" diameter × ½" long, the cove and bead area is ⁹⁄₁₆" diameter × ½" long, and the wheel hub area is ⅝" diameter × ¾" long. The saw slot is ⁵⁄₁₆" wide × ¾" deep.
- The wheel slot is ¼" wide × 1 ¹⁄₁₆" diameter. Use a length of ¹⁄₁₆" brass rod to drill and mount the wheels in place.
- Turn a small finial out of the dark wood to go on top of the canopy. Use a four-jaw chuck and turn the tenon ¼" by ¼". Use a bead and cove to look similar to the landing gear and make a pointed top.
- Also turn a hub for the propeller shaft. This can be turned like the wheels by drilling a ⅛" hole in the blank to fit on a piece of ⅛" dowel in the drill chuck. This is easier than drilling the finished turning.

Complete assembly by gluing the tail section in place. Sand and finish. Watch eyes light up as the music plays and the propeller turns. The wheels will even roll!

13

LIDDED BOX WITH PUSH-BUTTON MUSIC

This project is very similar to the next project, the "Traditional Turned Music Box," Project No. 14, in the technique that is required. The sequence in turning is the same except that whereas the lid is chucked onto the body, a separately turned disk of contrasting wood color is inserted in a cavity made to fit the insert.

An electronic battery-powered push-button music mechanism like the one that I used in this lidded box is available from many suppliers including Klockit (see page 51).

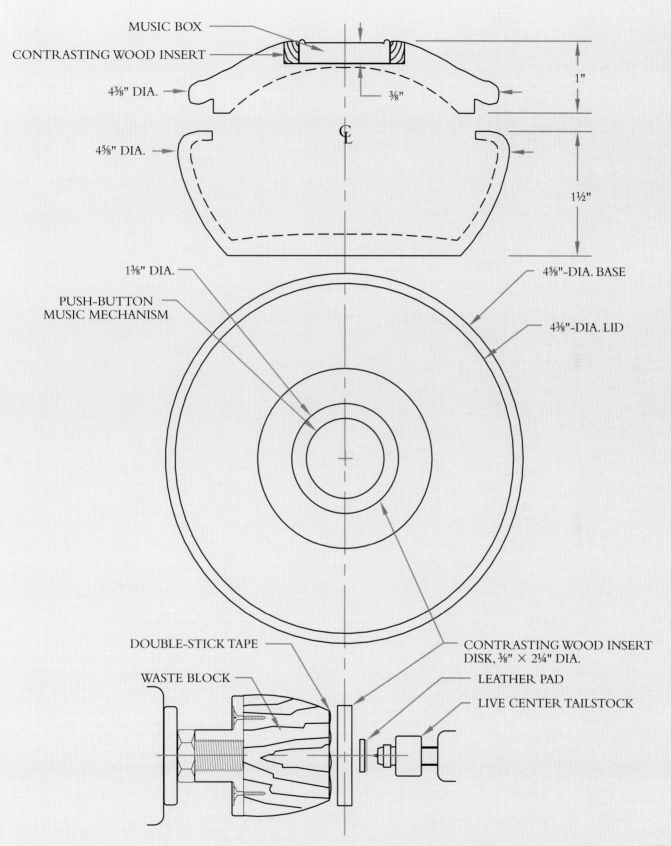

MUSIC BOX

CONTRASTING WOOD INSERT

4⅜" DIA.

⅜"

C̵L

1"

4⅝" DIA.

1½"

1⅜" DIA.

PUSH-BUTTON
MUSIC MECHANISM

4⅝"-DIA. BASE

4⅜"-DIA. LID

DOUBLE-STICK TAPE

WASTE BLOCK

CONTRASTING WOOD INSERT
DISK, ⅜" × 2¼" DIA.

LEATHER PAD

LIVE CENTER TAILSTOCK

VARIATIONS—

Should you wish, you can substitute the music mechanism with a disk of wood to have two colors in the lid. Multiple inlays are done in the same way.

Inlayed Patterns

Another suggestion for a variation is to use a center disk out of the same wood as the rest of the body, with an intervening contrasting circular band (see "Marquetry" on page 111). One person used a ring of PVC pipe inserted into a dark wood—it looked like an ivory insert.

Designing Your Own Boxes

Boxes, especially lidded boxes, are always fun to make and are prized as personal gifts and very sought after commercially by the general public and collectors. Try using some highly figured woods; these beautiful materials can produce some spectacular results. You can really enjoy this turning project by designing your own variations and making several different designs. The one with the music at the push of a button is still a favorite of mine and with many of the individuals who have come to possess one of these prized boxes.

As with everything else, the more you practice, the better you get, and the better the results will be.

Making the Lid

The cavities for both the contrasting wood and the music box are taken out with a parting tool making a straight cut into the lid. Note that the lid is left ½" thick to accommodate a ⅜"-thick disk and music mechanism.

Turning the Disk

❖ To turn the disk, use a waste block fastened onto a 3" faceplate. Turn the front of the waste block flat and smooth.
❖ Band-saw out a ⅜"-thick × 2¼"-diameter disk of contrasting wood color.
❖ Attach the disk to the waste block with double-stick carpet tape. Glue the disk in place with C/A glue.
❖ Use a pad that is made of wood or leather on the live center so that will not make a hole in the center of the disk.

The pressure of the tailstock will hold the disk in place so that it can be turned to the desired dimension. No sanding is necessary at this time on the disk. This will be done at the same time the rest of the lid is sanded and finished.

❖ Now, using the parting tool, turn a cavity in the disk 1⅜" diameter that will fit the music mechanism.

The electronic music mechanism should fit snug in the cavity in the lid but not too tight to be removed for battery replacement later. Do not glue the mechanism in place.

Finishing

To finish your lidded box, see "Sanding Suggestions" and "Finishes" earlier, on pages 8, 9, and 10.

14

TRADITIONAL TURNED MUSIC BOX

This original pattern utilizes a traditional music box with a brake lever. This kind of mechanism is available from many suppliers (see page 51).

Turning the Body

The body of the box is turned from a 5½"-diameter × 2¾" band-sawed blank that has been glued to a waste block mounted on a 3" faceplate. Use C/A glue to attach the blank to the waste block.

❖ With the tailstock live center in place for safety, turn the blank to a balanced cylinder. Turn the outside of the box to shape, then sand to a finish.

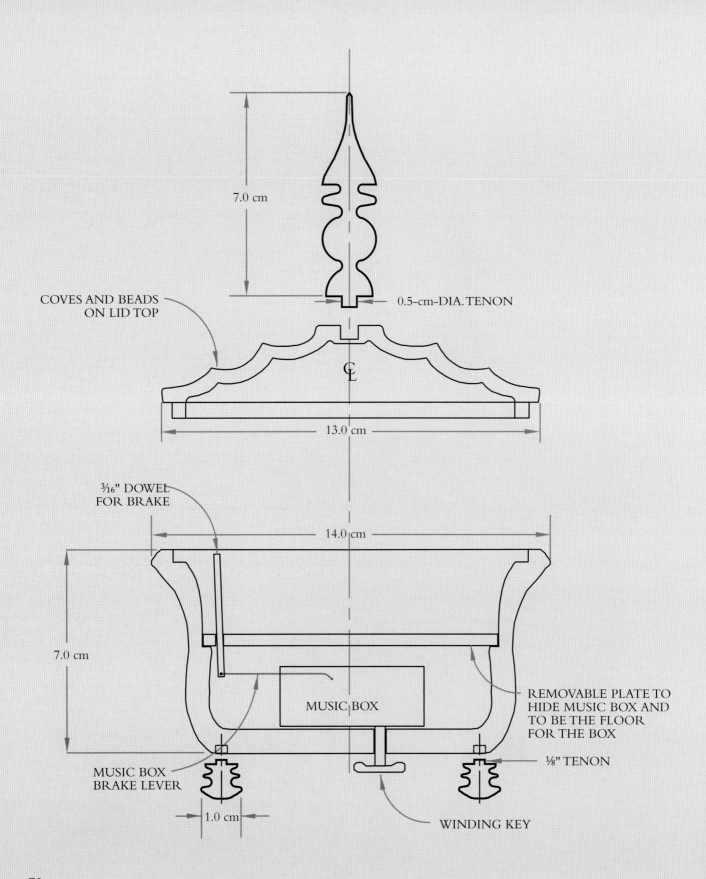

7.0 cm

COVES AND BEADS
ON LID TOP

0.5-cm-DIA. TENON

C̶L̶

13.0 cm

³⁄₁₆" DOWEL
FOR BRAKE

14.0 cm

7.0 cm

MUSIC BOX

REMOVABLE PLATE TO
HIDE MUSIC BOX AND
TO BE THE FLOOR
FOR THE BOX

MUSIC BOX
BRAKE LEVER

⅛" TENON

1.0 cm

WINDING KEY

- To turn the inside of the box, drill a ½"-diameter hole to the depth desired to serve as a depth gauge while you excavate the piece.
- With a parting tool, make the mortise groove in which the lid will fit. Excavate 1¼" deep and, with the parting tool, make the ledge that will hold the removable music-box cover plate.
- Check wall thickness with a figure-eight caliper to make certain that you do not get the wall too thin for the ledge.

Finish excavating the inside of the box. Sand and finish.(See "Sanding Suggestions" and "Finishes" earlier, on pages 8, 9, and 10.)

Index and mark the drill holes for the three feet at 120 degrees. (See the "Lathe Indexing" section earlier, on page 10.)

- Drill a ¼" hole in the lid blank and mount on a screw center or threaded-rod center as covered in Project No. 10. Check grain direction to get the best match between the lid and the body of the box.
- Turn the inside of the lid first. This allows access to check the fit of the lid to the body and will let you detail the inside.

Sand and finish the inside before removing and reversing to turn the outside. You can make coves and beads on the lid top as in the example or you may wish to leave it smooth.

Making the Cover
The removable music box cover plate is made on the waste block used earlier. Clean and flatten the face of the waste block so that you can use double-stick carpet tape. This tape is available at your local home improvements center or suppliers like Craft Supplies, USA (see page 26).

- Use the tailstock live center to hold the cover plate against the tape until you are finished turning. Two layers of leather between the plate and live center will keep it from marking the surface. A little pressure will hold the cover plate against the tape until

you are finished turning. The tape will hold well enough for the sanding process. Measure the ledge with calipers to insure a proper fit.

- Mark and drill a ⅛" hole in the cover plate to accommodate a ⅛" birch dowel that will be attached to the music box. A length of No. 12 brass wire will work as well should you prefer.
- With a drill press, drill holes in the bottom of the box for the three feet and the winding key. The music-box mechanism can be used as a template to locate the hole to be drilled for the winding key. See Project No. 10 for detailed instructions on turning the three feet.

Turning the Finial
- Turn the finial between centers using a ⅜" spur center and cup-type live center.
- Turn beads and coves on the small finial with a ½" skew.
- The ¼" tenon to be inserted in the top is made with a parting tool and measured with a set of calipers.

Use screw holes provided in the music box to secure the mechanism to the floor of the turning.

Do not use glue on the music mechanism. It may need replacing someday or you may want to change the tune.

Make sure that the winding-key shaft does not bind against the side of the drilled hole. It does not take very much friction to stop the key from turning.

- Feed the dowel that attaches to the music box through the cover plate.

Leave the dowel a little long so that it can be cut to fit against the lid. The lid will depress the dowel to stop the music when it is closed.

Enjoy Your Turning
Wind the key and present this project to your admirers with pride. It will become a valued family heirloom wherever it finds a home.

15 "LET THE GOOD TIMES ROLL" MUSIC BOX

This award-winning music box combines several types of turning procedure with optional carving and indexing skills. When the finial is wound, the music plays and a barely visible brass wire rolls nine ¾" turned wooden balls around inside the cage.

Hearts carved through the side allow the admirer to see the movement. As an alternative, a series of different-sized holes can be drilled for those who do not wish to carve. Being able to see through to the action is the fun part of this project.

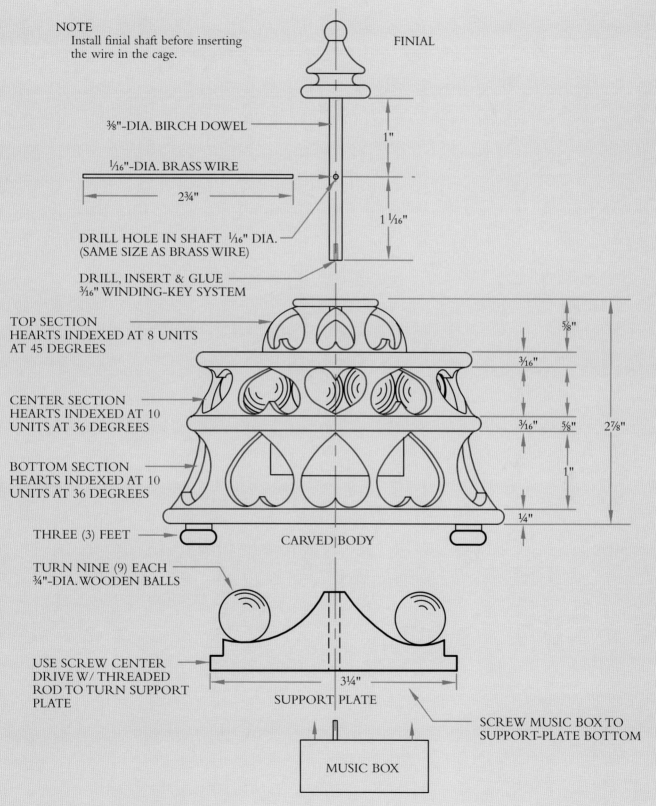

NOTE
Install finial shaft before inserting
the wire in the cage.

FINIAL

⅜"-DIA. BIRCH DOWEL

1"

1/16"-DIA. BRASS WIRE

2¾"

1 1/16"

DRILL HOLE IN SHAFT 1/16" DIA.
(SAME SIZE AS BRASS WIRE)

DRILL, INSERT & GLUE
3/16" WINDING-KEY SYSTEM

TOP SECTION
HEARTS INDEXED AT 8 UNITS
AT 45 DEGREES

5/8"

3/16"

CENTER SECTION
HEARTS INDEXED AT 10
UNITS AT 36 DEGREES

3/16" 5/8" 2⅞"

BOTTOM SECTION
HEARTS INDEXED AT 10
UNITS AT 36 DEGREES

1"

THREE (3) FEET

¼"

CARVED BODY

TURN NINE (9) EACH
¾"-DIA. WOODEN BALLS

USE SCREW CENTER
DRIVE W/ THREADED
ROD TO TURN SUPPORT
PLATE

3¼"

SUPPORT PLATE

SCREW MUSIC BOX TO
SUPPORT-PLATE BOTTOM

MUSIC BOX

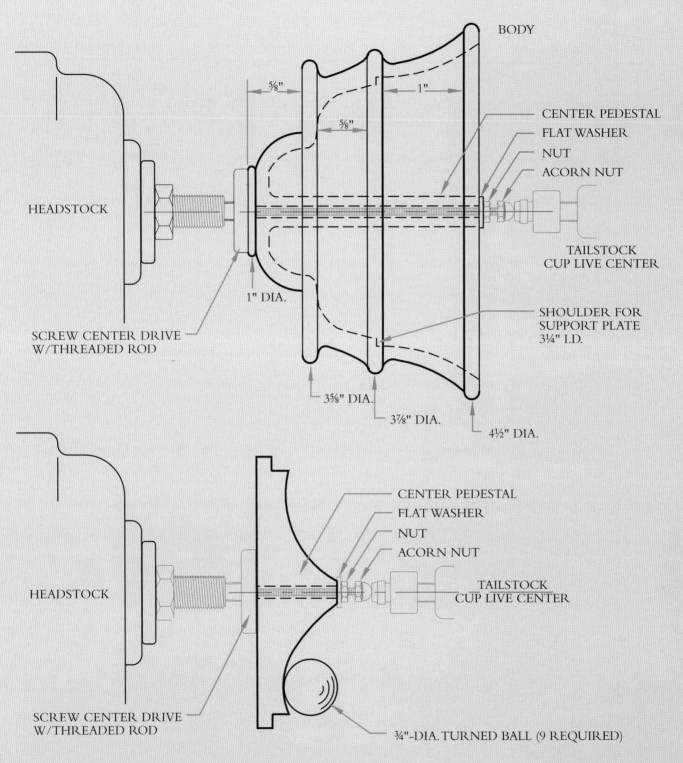

BODY

5/8"

1"

5/8"

CENTER PEDESTAL

FLAT WASHER

NUT

ACORN NUT

HEADSTOCK

TAILSTOCK
CUP LIVE CENTER

1" DIA.

SHOULDER FOR
SUPPORT PLATE
3¼" I.D.

SCREW CENTER DRIVE
W/THREADED ROD

3⅝" DIA.

3⅞" DIA.

4½" DIA.

CENTER PEDESTAL

FLAT WASHER

NUT

ACORN NUT

HEADSTOCK

TAILSTOCK
CUP LIVE CENTER

SCREW CENTER DRIVE
W/THREADED ROD

¾"-DIA. TURNED BALL (9 REQUIRED)

SUPPORT PLATE

TURNED SPHERE OR BALL

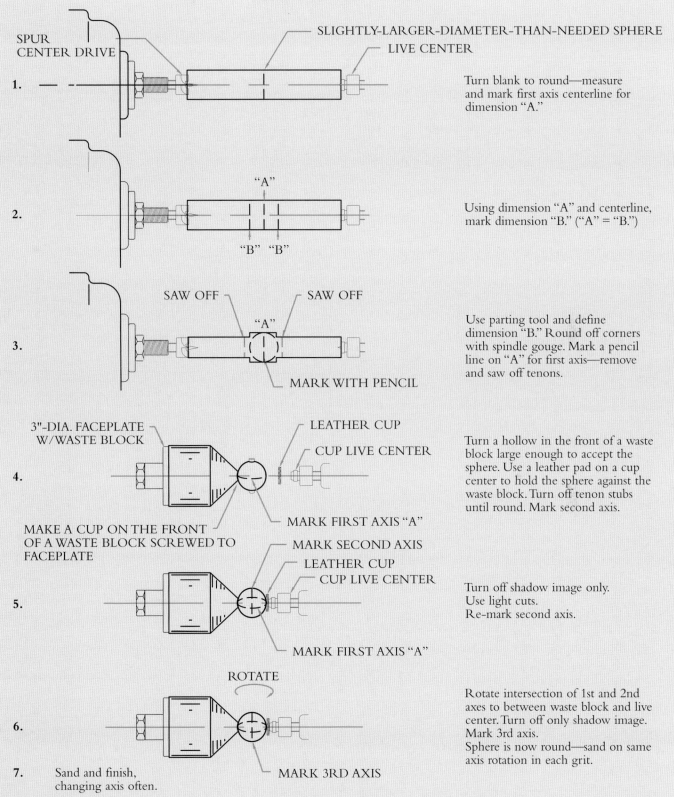

SPUR CENTER DRIVE

SLIGHTLY-LARGER-DIAMETER-THAN-NEEDED SPHERE

LIVE CENTER

1. Turn blank to round—measure and mark first axis centerline for dimension "A."

2. "A"
"B" "B"

Using dimension "A" and centerline, mark dimension "B." ("A" = "B.")

3. SAW OFF   SAW OFF
"A"
MARK WITH PENCIL

Use parting tool and define dimension "B." Round off corners with spindle gouge. Mark a pencil line on "A" for first axis—remove and saw off tenons.

4. 3"-DIA. FACEPLATE W/WASTE BLOCK
LEATHER CUP
CUP LIVE CENTER
MARK FIRST AXIS "A"
MAKE A CUP ON THE FRONT OF A WASTE BLOCK SCREWED TO FACEPLATE

Turn a hollow in the front of a waste block large enough to accept the sphere. Use a leather pad on a cup center to hold the sphere against the waste block. Turn off tenon stubs until round. Mark second axis.

5. MARK SECOND AXIS
LEATHER CUP
CUP LIVE CENTER
MARK FIRST AXIS "A"

Turn off shadow image only.
Use light cuts.
Re-mark second axis.

6. ROTATE
MARK 3RD AXIS

Rotate intersection of 1st and 2nd axes to between waste block and live center. Turn off only shadow image. Mark 3rd axis.
Sphere is now round—sand on same axis rotation in each grit.

7. Sand and finish, changing axis often.

Use a standard screw center or screw center with threaded rod (see drawings and Project No. 10) and mount the predrilled blank. Always use the tailstock with live center to support the project while roughing in until it is a balanced cylinder.

Pay close attention to wall thickness with figure-eight calipers. Use a spindle gouge or skew to turn the beads. In the example, skew lines are made on each side and down the center of each bead. (See Project No. 10 for indexing and turning the three feet for the bottom.)

TURNING THE SPHERES—

For those who would mistakenly avoid the fun of turning the spheres or balls, they are available already turned at most craft and hobby shops. The same sequence for turning small spheres works for larger diameters. Some spheres with highly figured crotch wood are beautiful as individual turnings. (See the drawings on page 75.)

Should you elect to purchase the ¾" wooden balls for this project, I suggest that before you install them, roll them, individually, carefully around, between the palms of your hands. That way you can keep with the tradition of absolute truthfulness of all turners. When someone asked if you turned the balls, you can say "Yes."

Finishing the Body

❖ Sand and finish the body while it is on the lathe. (See "Sanding Suggestions" and "Finishes" earlier, on pages 8, 9, and 10.) If you use the threaded-rod chuck, leave the center support in place until completed. Then, cut it off with a bench chisel. Using this chuck, the ¼" hole drilled for the rod will need to be reamed to ⅜" on both the body and support plate to accommodate the finial shaft that goes to the music box.

Preparing the Finial

The finial is turned between centers and can be turned in one piece or attached to a ⅜" birch dowel. However, it is best to turn it all out of the same wood so that the colors match.

❖ Drill a 3/16" hole in the bottom end of the finial shaft. Insert the threaded end of the winding key and glue in place with C/A glue.

This is necessary to attach the finial shaft to the threaded music box winding shaft. Music boxes are available from many suppliers (see page 51). Different lengths of winding key extensions are also available that can be used for this application rather than grinding the wings off of the winding key.

❖ Remove the cover from the music mechanism and screw the music box to the support plate through the holes provided. Make sure the finial shaft does not bind on the sides.

Assembly

❖ Drill a 1/16" hole in the finial shaft at the elevation of the centerline of the balls.
❖ With the piece assembled and the balls in place, insert through the hole a 1/16"-diameter × 2¾"-long length of brass wire. Do not glue in place.

In this example, the hearts are indexed at 8 units in the top—360 degrees divided by 8 equals 45-degree segments. The two carved areas in the side are indexed at 10 units—360 degrees divided by 10 equals 36 degrees each segment (see "Lathe Indexing" on pages 10 and 11).

Carving in this example was done primarily with a reversible, variable-speed mini-grinder. Holes were first drilled in the heart figures, then ground to the lines with a burr. A split mandrel with a small piece of sandpaper folded and inserted makes an excellent flap sander to finish the process. Always wear a dust mask and eye protection.

Perhaps you will want to take this project a step further and make two levels of rolling balls. Be creative—adapt the concepts in this project to make your own "Let the Good Times Roll!"

16 HORSE CAROUSEL MUSIC BOX

This intriguing music-box carousel project involves turning, carving, and some interesting engineering challenges. The drawings and plans will help give you ideas for a number of variations that you might make on this example.

The original concept was to try to utilize the power of the winding key to create movement and music at the same time (as we did with Project No. 11, described on page 57). Friction is the main problem to overcome when you are designing this type of project.

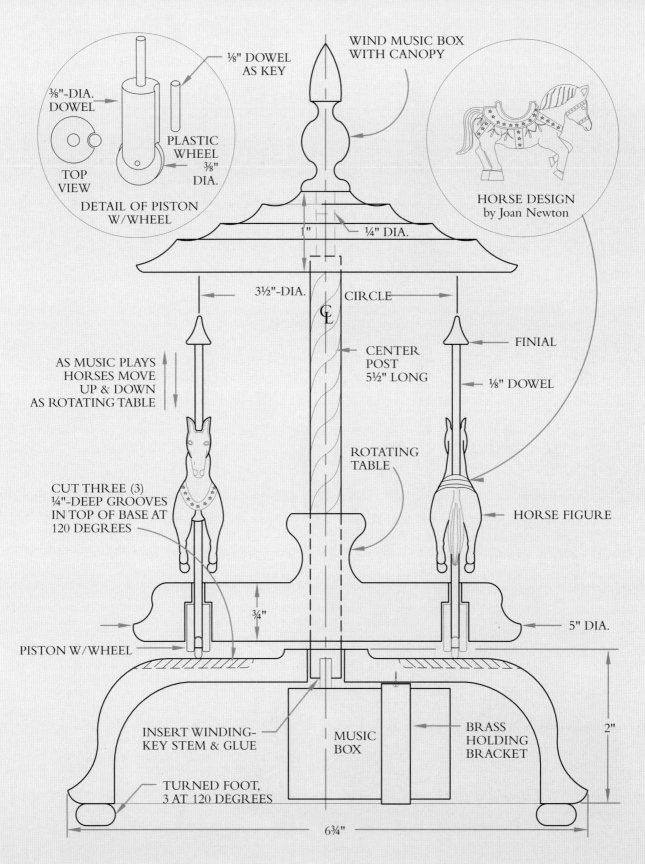

⅜"-DIA. DOWEL

⅛" DOWEL AS KEY

TOP VIEW

PLASTIC WHEEL ⅜" DIA.

DETAIL OF PISTON W/WHEEL

WIND MUSIC BOX WITH CANOPY

HORSE DESIGN
by Joan Newton

1"

¼" DIA.

3½"-DIA.   CIRCLE

C̶L

AS MUSIC PLAYS
HORSES MOVE
UP & DOWN
AS ROTATING TABLE

CENTER POST 5½" LONG

FINIAL

⅛" DOWEL

ROTATING TABLE

CUT THREE (3)
¼"-DEEP GROOVES
IN TOP OF BASE AT
120 DEGREES

HORSE FIGURE

¾"

5" DIA.

PISTON W/WHEEL

INSERT WINDING-
KEY STEM & GLUE

MUSIC BOX

BRASS HOLDING BRACKET

2"

TURNED FOOT,
3 AT 120 DEGREES

6¾"

Preparing the Base

❖ Turn the base on a standard screw center or screw center with a threaded rod as in Project No. 10.

The drilled hole in the center can be reamed to fit the center post later—leave ample thickness in the top of the base to sand in the waves that will make the horses go up and down. A half-inch thickness will allow plenty of wood to sand in the ¼" grooves.

❖ Use the wheel or rounded end of the belt sander with an aggressive grit to sand in the three grooves ¼" deep at 120 degrees.

These should have a gentle slope so that the music box motor will have enough power to rotate the canopy.

❖ Hand sanding and polishing this surface is important to reduce friction.
❖ Index for three feet at 120 degrees. See Project No. 18 for details of turning the feet.
❖ Drill ³⁄₁₆" holes ¼" deep in the edge of the base that will hold the feet.

Making the Rotating Assembly

❖ Turn the rotating table on the same set up as above.
❖ On the bottom of the rotating table, index for seven carousel horse assemblies—360 degrees divided by 7 equals 51½ degrees.
❖ Drill ⅛" holes through the table from the bottom, on a 3½" circle. Using the ⅛" hole as a guide, drill ⅜" holes ½" deep.
❖ With a ⅛" veinor chisel carve a ⅛"-wide groove ¹⁄₁₆" deep at the same quadrant in each of the drilled holes. (See the drawing.)

This groove is for the ⅛" dowel that will act as a guide to keep the horses rolling forward. The music box winds clockwise so the horses will go counterclockwise. Position them to ride in a forward motion.

❖ Cut seven pieces of ⅜" dowel ¾" long to be pistons to move the horses up and down.
❖ Drill a ⅛" hole ³⁄₁₆" deep in the top of each piston for the vertical shafts that will carry the horses.
❖ Saw a slot in the bottom of the piston ⅛" wide × ¼" deep for the wheel.

❖ Cut a groove in the piston with the ⅛" veinor chisel used earlier to match the one in the side of the ⅜" drill hole to keep the horses straight.

Obtain from the local hobby shop (or make your own) ⅜" plastic or nylon wheel ⅛" wide. Use a ¹⁄₆₄" brass wire to mount the wheel in the bottom of the piston. This wheel will roll over the indentations ground in the top of the base to make the carousel horse assembly go up and down. This assembly must move up and down in the drill hole without binding or the music mechanism will not power the canopy around.

THE CAROUSEL HORSES—

The horses, designed originally by Joan Newton, of Lampasas, Texas, are carved and detailed with a woodburner. Whatever figures you choose to use are mounted on a ⅛" dowel 2½" long inserted in the hole drilled in the top of each piston. A small turned finial should be made to top each dowel.

The center support post can be a ⅜" dowel or decorated spindle turning. Grind the extensions off the winding key until it is ³⁄₁₆" round. Drill a hole in the bottom of the support post and glue the key stem in place with C/A glue.

The winding shaft inside the motor of the music box is threaded to fit the winding key. By inserting the key stub in the shaft, it can be screwed into the music box to support the canopy. The music mechanism is secured under the base with a thin ⅜" brass strap in a "U" shape and screwed against the underside of the base.

The canopy is turned on the same system as the rotating table and base. Ream the underside of the hole to fit the top of the center support post.

The finial is turned between centers or in a four-jaw chuck. Use calipers to size the tenon to fit the hole in the canopy. Glue the finial and center post to the canopy with C/A glue. Make sure that the canopy is level.

17 FLYING BIRDS CAROUSEL MUSIC BOX

BIRD GO ROUND
S. GARY ROBERTS

Lift the canopy slightly, wind the knob, release both, and watch the birds fly to the tune of a music box.

This project is the result of wanting to have the winding key separate from the rotating mobile of carved birds suspended on thread. The winding key is a turned knob and connects to a miniature sheave that drives a drive belt. The belt, in turn, rotates the canopy to make the birds fly. Choose what you want to hang from the canopy—airplanes, turned balloons, or something else.

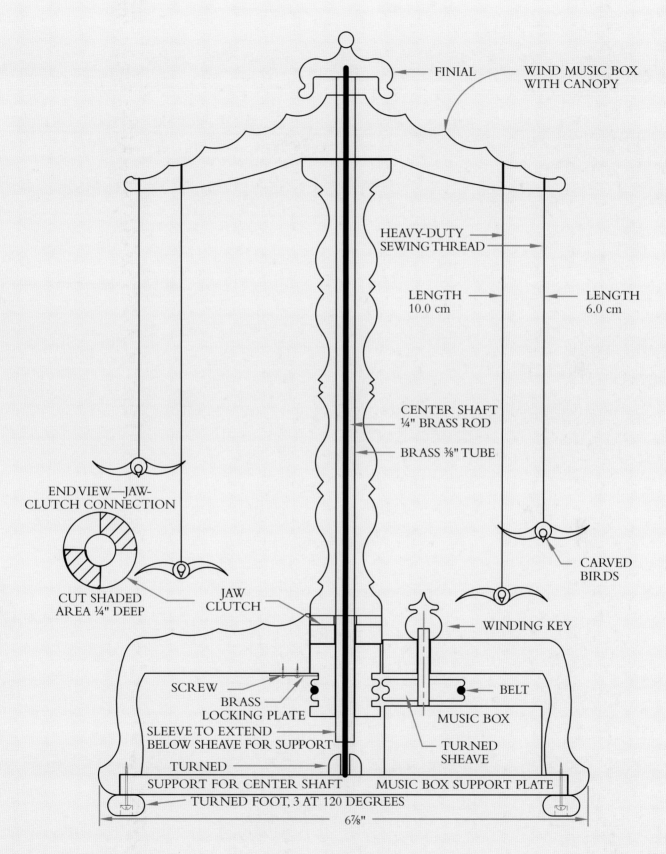

FINIAL

WIND MUSIC BOX
WITH CANOPY

HEAVY-DUTY
SEWING THREAD

LENGTH
10.0 cm

LENGTH
6.0 cm

CENTER SHAFT
¼" BRASS ROD

BRASS ⅜" TUBE

END VIEW—JAW-
CLUTCH CONNECTION

CARVED
BIRDS

CUT SHADED
AREA ¼" DEEP

JAW
CLUTCH

WINDING KEY

SCREW

BELT

BRASS
LOCKING PLATE

MUSIC BOX

SLEEVE TO EXTEND
BELOW SHEAVE FOR SUPPORT

TURNED
SHEAVE

TURNED

SUPPORT FOR CENTER SHAFT   MUSIC BOX SUPPORT PLATE

TURNED FOOT, 3 AT 120 DEGREES

6⅞"

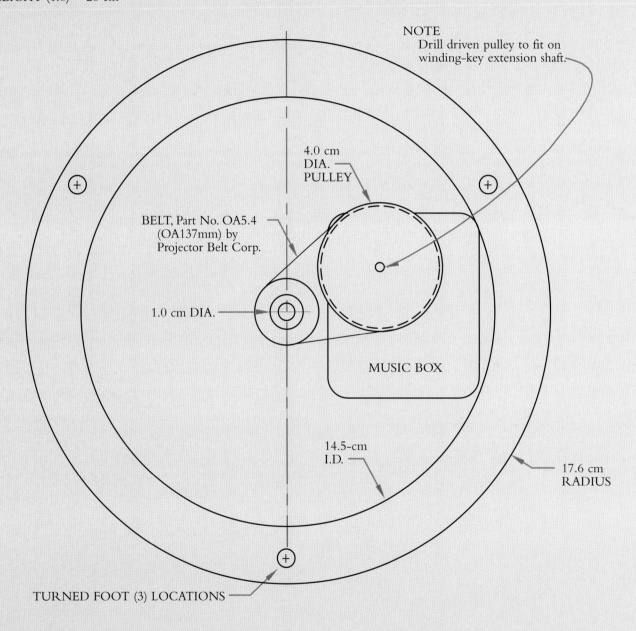

1.0 × 1.6

DIAMETER (1.0) = 17.6 cm
HEIGHT (1.6) = 28 cm

NOTE
Drill driven pulley to fit on
winding-key extension shaft.

4.0 cm
DIA.
PULLEY

BELT, Part No. OA5.4
(OA137mm) by
Projector Belt Corp.

1.0 cm DIA.

MUSIC BOX

14.5-cm
I.D.

17.6 cm
RADIUS

TURNED FOOT (3) LOCATIONS

Preparing the Pieces

❖ The base is turned as described in Project No. 10 (on page 54) out of a 2½"-thick × 7" band-sawed blank. The center hole is redrilled after turning to 1" diameter.

❖ The music box support plate is turned using double-stick carpet tape on a waste block. Music boxes are available from many suppliers (see page 51).

❖ The finial and winding key are both drilled before turning with a ¼" hole ¼" deep. A short piece of ¼" dowel in a Jacobs chuck in the headstock will serve as a mandrel to turn the pieces.

A leather pad on a small cup-type live center holds the piece in place for turning. The 1½" sheave on the winding key is also made on the same setup.

❖ The ¾"-diameter powered sheave is turned on a short piece of the ⅜" dowel mounted with the same method as the finial.

❖ The canopy is turned from a 1"-thick × 6¼"-diameter band-sawed blank, then the center hole is reamed to ⅜" with a Forstner bit after turning.

The drive belt I used is available at most electronic repair parts warehouses—it is Part No. OA5.4 manufactured by Projector Belt Corp. Buy a spare and enclose it with the mechanism in case someone later needs a new belt—leave it in the original package so the future owner will have that reference number for further replacements.

The Support Column

❖ The center support column is made from a 1½" × 1½" × 6¼" blank with the center drilled out. Use a four-jaw chuck and predrill with a ⅜" electrician's bit (they are 18" long), held in the Jacobs chuck in the tailstock.

Drilling the hole first eliminates trying to drill a hole in the thin-wall turning.

❖ After the hole is drilled, use a short piece of ⅜" brass tubing or dowel in the Jacobs chuck in the headstock and a small cone in the live center and turn as you would any spindle.

Make the top end flange 1¼" in diameter. Turn the bottom flange 1" in diameter by ¾" long so that you can make the jaws for the jaw clutch (see drawings).

WINDING "JAW CLUTCH"—

To connect and disconnect the canopy for winding purposes so the bird threads will not tangle from being turned backwards, it is necessary to make a quick-disconnect connection called a "jaw clutch."

The top end of the sheave and the bottom end of the center support column are made so that they will interlock.

❖ The brass rod that connects to the finial is ⁵⁄₁₆" longer than necessary to allow the canopy to be lifted ¼" during the winding cycle to disengage the jaw clutch. See drawing for jaw clutch connection.

❖ A groove on the underside of the jaw clutch is ¹⁄₁₆" wide and is used to hold the sheave in place by means of a small brass plate screwed into the roof of the base.

The lower end of the brass rod rests unattached in a drilled cup to maintain the alignment of the canopy. Coat the rod with graphite to reduce friction. A small ball bearing or BB placed in a shallow hole in the end of the rod can also be used to reduce friction.

If the belt tends to slip, a bit of beeswax will solve the problem. After it has played a few times, the action will get smoother and the music lasts longer. Friction in the least amount can stall the tiny motor in the music box.

The birds were hung from various lengths of heavy-duty sewing thread that matched the color of the wood. The point of an awl created the hole in which C/A glue was used to secure the thread.

Lift the canopy slightly, wind the music box, and lower the canopy to engage the jaw clutch. Watch the birds soar to the music as they would on a clear sunny day!

18 THREAD DISPENSER WITH HIDDEN DRAWER

This project was designed by my wife—as were several others. What better design source than the one who determines the need? She asked for a project that would allow a stack of spools at four corners and I added the round shape with the pincushion on top.

The hidden drawer was incorporated as a little surprise. Leo Doyle, the Californian, who was the first vice president of the American Association of Woodturners, showed me how to make hidden compartments in 1986. Thanks to Leo, I have included them in several of my own designs.

Choose a hard wood with good lateral-grain strength such as maple, mesquite, walnut, or mahogany.

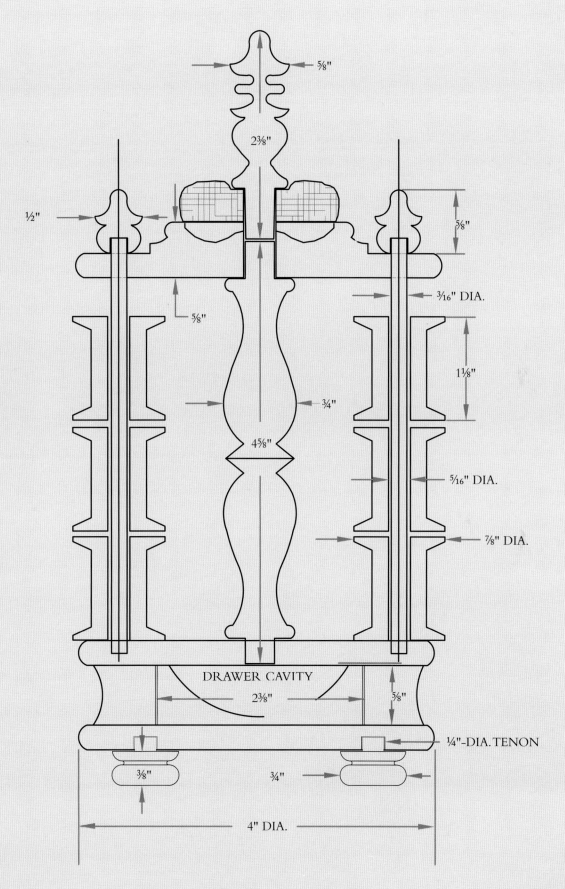

5⁄8"

2³⁄8"

½"

5⁄8"

5⁄8"

³⁄16" DIA.

1¹⁄8"

¾"

4⁵⁄8"

⁵⁄16" DIA.

⁷⁄8" DIA.

DRAWER CAVITY

2³⁄8"

5⁄8"

¼"-DIA. TENON

³⁄8"

¾"

4" DIA.

HIDDEN DRAWER BASE BEFORE TURNING

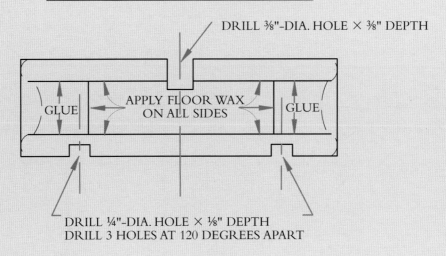

DRILL ⅜"-DIA. HOLE × ⅜" DEPTH

GLUE

APPLY FLOOR WAX ON ALL SIDES

GLUE

DRILL ¼"-DIA. HOLE × ⅛" DEPTH
DRILL 3 HOLES AT 120 DEGREES APART

TURNING FEET

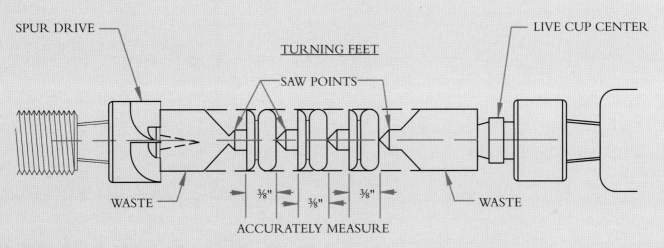

SPUR DRIVE

LIVE CUP CENTER

SAW POINTS

WASTE

WASTE

⅜"   ⅜"   ⅜"

ACCURATELY MEASURE

USING THE DRILL CHUCK AS A MANDEL

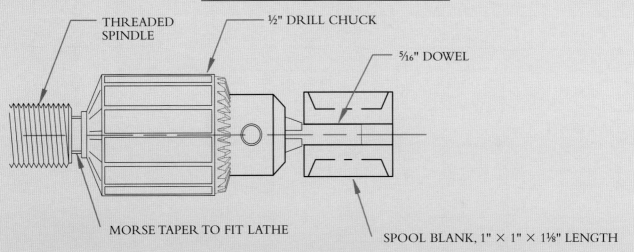

THREADED SPINDLE

½" DRILL CHUCK

5/16" DOWEL

MORSE TAPER TO FIT LATHE

SPOOL BLANK, 1" × 1" × 1⅛" LENGTH

Making the Pieces

❖ The legs are indexed at 120 degrees to give the piece stability and raise it off of the table. Turn the legs from a scrap of the project wood using a four-jaw chuck. The tenon can be a convenient diameter but the height needs to be a precise height measurement so that all three are the same.

I always use three legs to avoid the tedious adjustments to make four legs the exact same height.

❖ Make the top finial to your own design. This is a good place to show your skills at beads and coves. Leave a long shank to extend through the pincushion to enable you to glue it into the canopy. The center support post is made the same way.

❖ For the finials on top of the spool spindle rods, pre-drill the blocks to the same size as the ³⁄₁₆" dowels to be used to support the spools. Then, using a short piece of dowel in the headstock-mounted drill chuck held in place by a cup-type live center, turn each finial.

Preparing the Canopy

The canopy is first band-sawed round and drilled with the same size bit as the tenon on the center support. Place a short piece of dowel of the correct size in the drill chuck. This will serve as a mandrel on which to turn the canopy piece. Use the tailstock live center to create friction and stability while turning. The center part under the live center that you cannot remove while turning can be easily removed with a bench chisel. It is not necessary to sand the area that will be covered by the pincushion.

Making the Base

If you make the project the same size as this example, index the seven holes at 52.3 degrees, the same as those in the canopy. The drill circle should be ½" in from the outer edge. This will allow room for spools to be removed and replaced.

The base contains a hidden compartment or drawer to hold a very small pair of scissors to be used to cut threads. This is the fun surprise part of the project and one that you may want to include in other designs.

The base contains five parts. I used a table saw and a good blade that left a very smooth surface to cut out the pieces from the same piece of stock. Before you start, use a piece of masking tape on each piece to determine later where it goes back so that the grain will match. Do not remove any more wood in the kerf than is necessary to maximize graining match.

❖ The centerpiece is completely coated with a heavy coat of paste wax before the other pieces are glued and clamped in place. After it is turned, the center block can be driven out with a soft-surfaced dowel.

❖ Drill a hole with a Forstner bit through the top and about ⅛" into the block that will become the hidden compartment. Use the same dowel in the drill chuck that was used to turn the canopy. This will hold everything together while turning.

❖ Once the drawer is removed, it can then be hollowed with a chisel and the hollow can be hand sanded. After the wax is cleaned from the sliding surfaces of the drawer you will find that it fits well and can be removed from either direction.

THE PINCUSHION—

The pincushion is made from velvet or velour that can be purchased from the remnant table at most fabric stores. To get the correct size, measure the cavity diameter and draw a circle on a scrap of paper twice that size to be used as a pattern.

Make a pouch using needle and thread to weave in and out stitches around the outside of the circle of fabric. Leave long ends for pulling the threads to form the pouch.

Use quilt batting or cotton for stuffing. Push the stuffing in the center and pull the threads. It will form a pouch for the stuffing and can be flattened and shaped to fit the cavity.

Tie the end of the threads when the desired shape is obtained. Use an awl to make the center hole for the finial.

WOODEN SPOOLS—

Spools will turn easily and quickly using this method.

❖ Saw out 21 blocks 1⅛" long (with the grain) by 1" square. Using the drill press, drill a ⁵⁄₁₆" hole with the grain.
❖ Cut a ⁵⁄₁₆" dowel long enough to protrude from the chuck about ¾".

Mount it in the previously used Jacobs chuck as a mandrel. Pressure from the live center will create enough friction to turn the blank.

❖ Place the spool blank on the tenon and secure in place with a large pointed live center on the tailstock. Turn at about 2,000 rpm.

If your lathe is equipped with a hand wheel on the tailstock, you can—with caution—use the procedure that I learned from Rude Osolnik of leaving the lathe running.

❖ I use a ½" skew chisel to turn to round then make 45 degree cuts about ⅛" in from each end of the spool, then take out the center.
❖ Without turning the lathe off, I retract the live center by use of the handwheel which will allow the spool to stop spinning and be removed from the tenon.
❖ Slide on the next block and with the hand wheel, advance the live center to create friction on the tenon and waste block.

Make sure that you release the block BEFORE it starts to spin or you can create a serious injury to your fingers by their being trapped between the block and the tool rest. Use caution! This procedure should be approached cautiously and only by experienced turners.

❖ Insert the finial and use C/A glue to hold both the pincushion and finial in place. Lay the canopy on top of the base and, using a dowel in the center hole to center one over the other, align the grain so that the top and base match.
❖ Now mark the holes for drilling the base. Make sure you do not drill too deep and ruin the function of the hidden drawer. All holes should be drilled in a drill press to assure accuracy. Attempting to hand-drill holes can produce unfortunate results.

Making Spools

Why not make your project look really great by turning your own matching wooden spools? See "Wooden Spools" in the sidebar and "A Set of Spools" on page 100. Once you have mastered this technique, you will enjoy the speed at which you can produce the finished product.

Final Touches

For sanding and finishing see "Sanding Suggestions" and "Finishes" earlier, on pages 8, 9, and 10.

Now that you have the tidy (see page 93) and spools finished, there are two more things you should add before you sign the piece.

❖ A pincushion should always have pins. Pick up an assortment of pins with colorful heads. Place a few pins in the cushion.
❖ Spools should always have thread on them. Pick up an assortment of different colors of thread. Make a knife cut at the edge of the spool, with the grain, to hold the thread end.
❖ Mount the new spool on a dowel in a variable-speed drill. Masking tape around the dowel provides a grip on the spool. With the source spool of thread on a loose-fitting dowel held in the vise, spin on a few layers of thread to add color to the finished product. Go slowly or you can create a colorful mess.

Now you can sign, date, and put the name of the wood on the bottom of the piece. It will become a family heirloom appreciated by others, and you had the pleasure and privilege of creating it with your own skills.

19 SEWING TIDY WITH THIMBLE

This is a fun project that will require about half a day's lathe time. Now, don't write me if it does not take that long or if it takes perhaps a little bit longer. Just enjoy the challenge of doing a precision turning project.

To prepare the blank for turning, use your band saw to cut out a 6"-long × 1¾"-diameter cylinder from good straight-grained hardwood. If your band saw does not have enough height to do this, then turn a cylinder using a spur center.

TURNING SEQUENCE

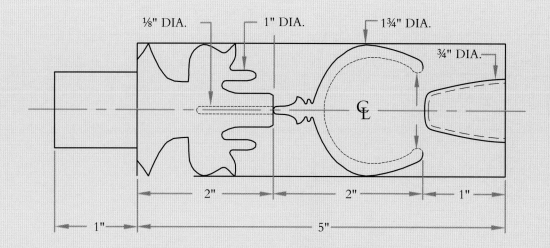

⅛" DIA. 1" DIA. 1¾" DIA. ¾" DIA.

C̶L

2" 2" 1"

1" 5"

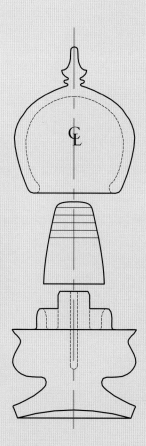

C̶L

ASSEMBLY SEQUENCE

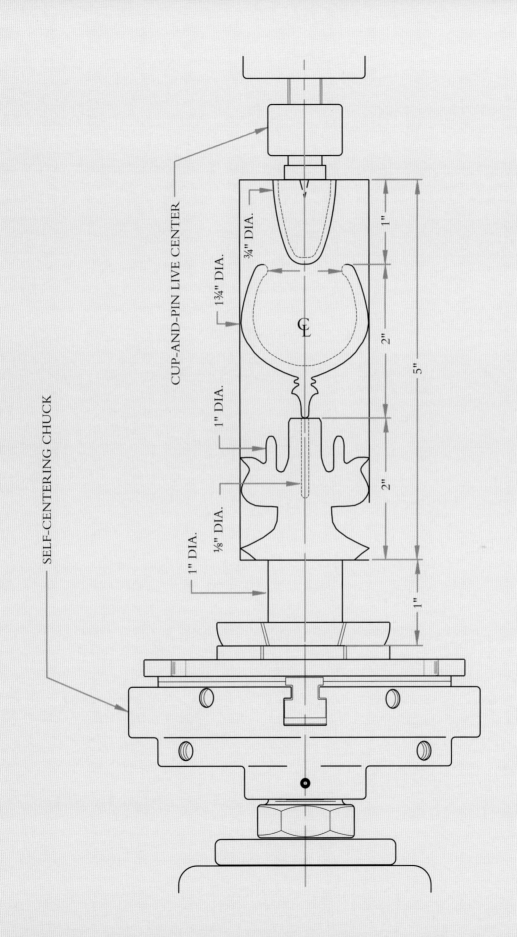

CUP-AND-PIN LIVE CENTER

SELF-CENTERING CHUCK

¾" DIA.

1¾" DIA.

1" DIA.

⅛" DIA.

1" DIA.

1"

2"

5"

2"

1"

C̵L

TURNING THE PIECES—

Use the tailstock to help center and secure the turning in a four-jaw chuck. For those of you that have not added this wonderful convenience, add 1" to the length of the blank and turn a 1" tenon 1" long on one end and glue it into a drilled hole in a waste block. Either way, the cylinder needs to be stable for this project.

1. After mounting, true up the outside of the cylinder.
2. To turn the thimble, use a drill chuck mounted in the tailstock, and drill a ⅜"-diameter hole in the end, ¾" deep.
3. With a small ¼" roundnose chisel, taper the hole from the bottom to ⅝" inside diameter on the outer edge. Vary this if you are making the thimble for someone in particular—just measure their finger.
4. Run up a cone-type live center mounted in the tailstock to hold the cylinder steady.

Do not force the cone into the wood, just tighten enough to hold it in perfect center. Too much pressure can split the wood.

5. Now, bring the thimble into shape with a good sharp skew. Leave about a ³⁄₁₆" tenon until you have put in a few skew lines near the closed end of the thimble, then cut it off with the toe of the skew.
6. Next, make the top cover for the project. This is made using the same procedure you would use to make a goblet.
7. Use a ½" drill bit and drill to the depth of the cup. Leave a little room to sand the bottom. This will act as a depth gauge to let you know when you are deep enough.

Hollow out the cup and be sure not to make the opening too wide. This will be where the top and base fit together. Check your measurements carefully. Sand and finish the inside of the hollow.

8. Bring up the cone again on the tailstock and, without great pressure, stabilize the turning.
9. Now, you can turn the outside of the top. Stop often and check to make sure you have a consistent wall thickness.
10. Once this is done, you can create a finial. With the project stable between centers, you can shape the finial to suit your artistic eye.
11. Sand and apply the finish before parting off with a skew (see "Sanding Suggestions" and "Finishes" earlier, on pages 8, 9, and 10).

Next in line on the blank will be the base.

12. Drill a ³⁄₁₆" hole about 1" deep. This will be for storing needles and pins and could be smaller if you wish.
13. With a ⅛" wide parting tool, cut a groove next to the pinhole, leaving about a ⅜"-diameter pedestal in the center. Widen it slightly until the thimble fits into the outside of the groove. This should fit like a lidded box—nice and snug. Once it is fitted to the thimble, do not sand this area.
14. Start at the outside of the cylinder with your parting tool making end-grain cuts, then fit the lid to the base. Remove the wood carefully, making light cuts until the top slides on and fits snugly.
15. Again, bring up the tailstock to support the turning and shape the base. I used a small shop-made ¹⁄₁₆" roundnose chisel to make the small coves. If you do not have one, a concrete nail in a dowel or an old screwdriver can be ground into a very useful tool.

Make the base slightly concave so that it can sit steadily on a table. If you would like to embellish the bottom of the turning, you should have enough wood left in the chuck to make a jam chuck.

❖ Turn a nice fit with your parting tool, reverse the base, and push the lid-fit tenon of the base into the chuck.
❖ This will allow you access to the base for sanding and decoration. A little chatter work between skew lines is always impressive.

Make another right away and enjoy turning!

SPOOL TIDY

The urge to keep a bunch of related items together, in some order and readily accessible, inevitably leads to the search for a solution. Build a special holder. Today, we call such a holder an organizer; 150 years ago it would have been known as a tidy. That is why I called this antique-looking thread-spool caddy that I designed a "Spool Tidy."

Constructing the tidy calls for three faceplate turnings and five spindle turnings. A set of spools adds eight more spindle turnings.

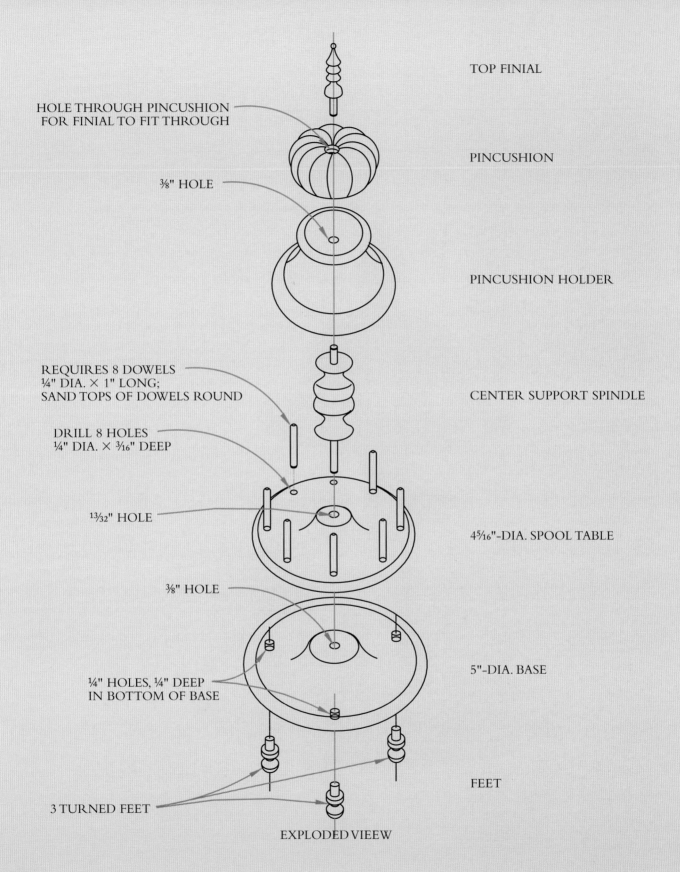

TOP FINIAL

HOLE THROUGH PINCUSHION
FOR FINIAL TO FIT THROUGH

PINCUSHION

⅜" HOLE

PINCUSHION HOLDER

REQUIRES 8 DOWELS
¼" DIA. × 1" LONG;
SAND TOPS OF DOWELS ROUND

CENTER SUPPORT SPINDLE

DRILL 8 HOLES
¼" DIA. × ³⁄₁₆" DEEP

¹³⁄₃₂" HOLE

4⁵⁄₁₆"-DIA. SPOOL TABLE

⅜" HOLE

5"-DIA. BASE

¼" HOLES, ¼" DEEP
IN BOTTOM OF BASE

FEET

3 TURNED FEET

EXPLODED VIEEW

94

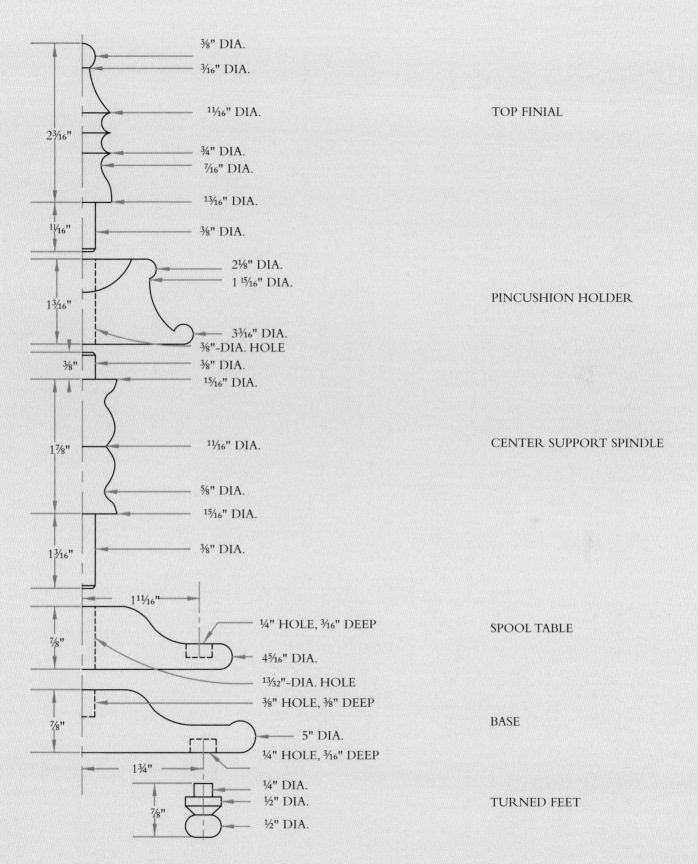

⅜" DIA.

³⁄₁₆" DIA.

¹¹⁄₁₆" DIA.

2³⁄₁₆"

¾" DIA.

⁷⁄₁₆" DIA.

¹³⁄₁₆" DIA.

1¹⁄₁₆"

⅜" DIA.

2⅛" DIA.

1 ¹⁵⁄₁₆" DIA.

1³⁄₁₆"

3³⁄₁₆" DIA.

⅜"-DIA. HOLE

⅜"

⅜" DIA.

¹⁵⁄₁₆" DIA.

1⁷⁄₈"

¹¹⁄₁₆" DIA.

⅝" DIA.

¹⁵⁄₁₆" DIA.

1³⁄₁₆"

⅜" DIA.

1¹¹⁄₁₆"

¼" HOLE, ³⁄₁₆" DEEP

⅞"

4⁵⁄₁₆" DIA.

¹³⁄₃₂"-DIA. HOLE

⅜" HOLE, ⅜" DEEP

⅞"

5" DIA.

¼" HOLE, ³⁄₁₆" DEEP

1¾"

¼" DIA.

½" DIA.

⅞"

½" DIA.

TOP FINIAL

PINCUSHION HOLDER

CENTER SUPPORT SPINDLE

SPOOL TABLE

BASE

TURNED FEET

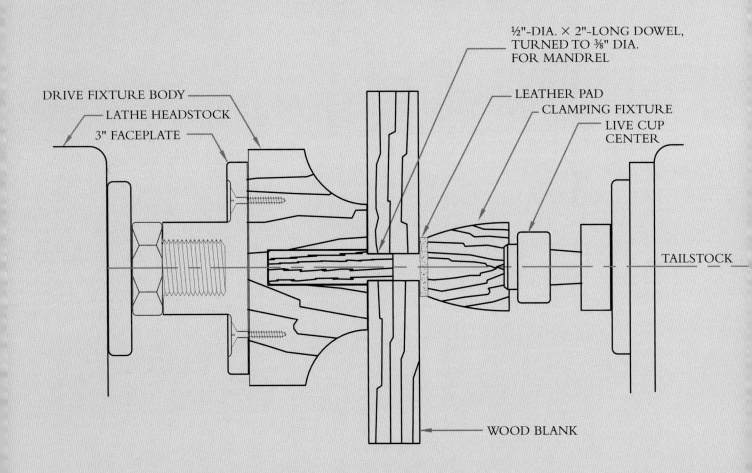

½"-DIA. × 2"-LONG DOWEL,
TURNED TO ⅜" DIA.
FOR MANDREL

DRIVE FIXTURE BODY

LATHE HEADSTOCK

3" FACEPLATE

LEATHER PAD

CLAMPING FIXTURE

LIVE CUP
CENTER

TAILSTOCK

WOOD BLANK

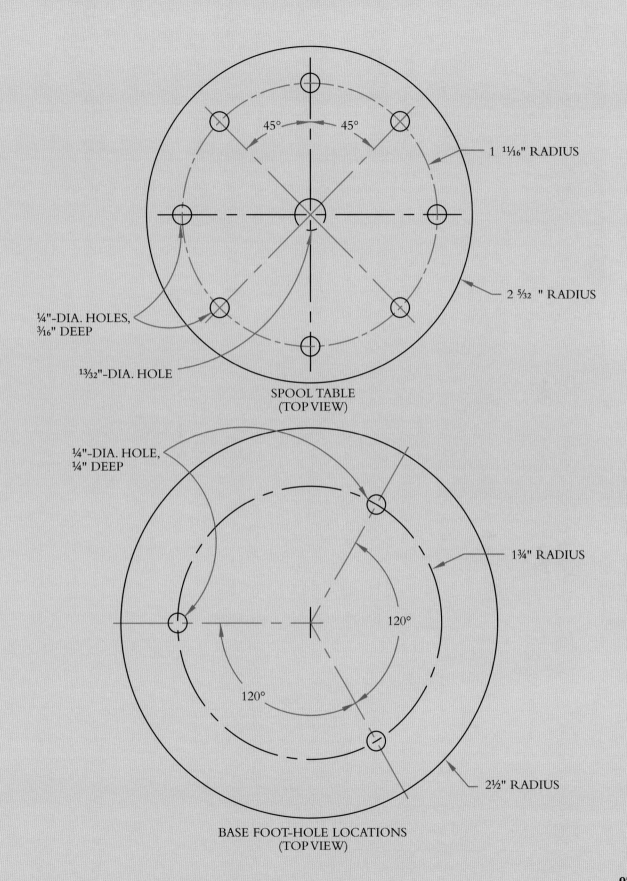

45° 45°

1 ¹¹⁄₁₆" RADIUS

2 ⁵⁄₃₂ " RADIUS

¼"-DIA. HOLES,
³⁄₁₆" DEEP

¹³⁄₃₂"-DIA. HOLE

SPOOL TABLE
(TOP VIEW)

¼"-DIA. HOLE,
¼" DEEP

1¾" RADIUS

120°

120°

2½" RADIUS

BASE FOOT-HOLE LOCATIONS
(TOP VIEW)

MANDREL FIXTURE

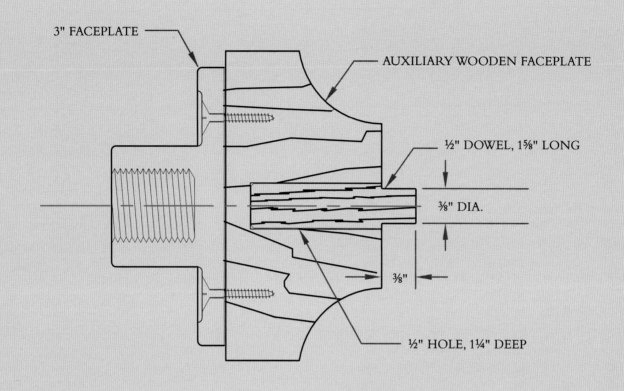

3" FACEPLATE

AUXILIARY WOODEN FACEPLATE

½" DOWEL, 1⅝" LONG

⅜" DIA.

⅜"

½" HOLE, 1¼" DEEP

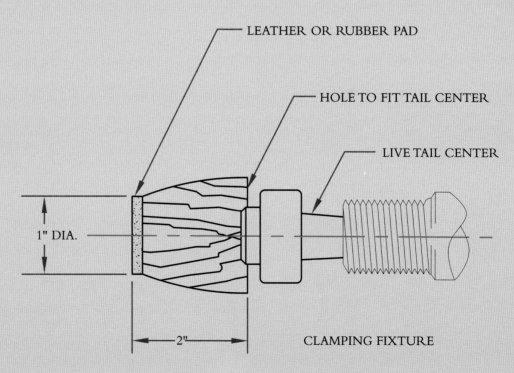

LEATHER OR RUBBER PAD

HOLE TO FIT TAIL CENTER

LIVE TAIL CENTER

1" DIA.

2"

CLAMPING FIXTURE

Making the Mandrel

❖ To build a mandrel fixture, start by band-sawing a scrap wood disk about 1½" thick to fit the 3" faceplate for your lathe.

❖ Attach the disk to the faceplate with 1¼" wood screws. This will be the body for the drive fixture.

❖ Turn the body round, and true the face.

❖ Bore a ½" hole 1¼" deep straight into the center of the face with a small gouge. You also could bore the hole with a drill bit held in a tailstock-mounted chuck.

❖ Glue a 2" length of ½" dowel into the hole.

After the glue dries, turn the protruding dowel (the mandrel) to ⅜" diameter. Part off the end at ⅜" as shown in the mandrel-fixture drawing. Turn the body to the profile shown, leaving a flat face about 1½" in diameter around the mandrel.

❖ To make the clamping fixture, which will hold the workpiece against the mandrel fixture, bore one end of a piece of scrap wood with a hole that fits over your lathe's live tail center.

❖ Turn the piece between centers, bringing it to ¾" diameter at a point about 2" from the tailstock.

❖ Part off the 2" section.

Glue a piece of leather to the flat end as shown in the clamping fixture drawing. The resilient leather will help prevent marring the turning. Press the clamping fixture onto the live tail center, as shown, and mount the mandrel fixture on the headstock.

Turning the Base and Table

❖ Band-saw two disks from 1" thick stock, one 5½" diameter, the other 5".

❖ With a ⅜" bit, drill a hole through the center of the small blank and one ⅜" deep into the center of the large blank.

❖ On the other side of the large blank, locate and drill the three holes for the feet, as in the base drawing.

Fit the center hole in the large blank over the mandrel. Bring up the tailstock with the live center and clamping fixture installed. With the tailstock, press the blank snugly against the mandrel fixture, as shown in the drawing. You do not need to clamp it too tightly.

USING A MANDREL—

A shop-made mandrel fixture allows you to mount the blanks for the tidy's three faceplate turnings, production style, without gluing them to a faceplate. Here is how it works.

❖ A short pin or tenon (the mandrel) extends from the face of the drive fixture, which is mounted on the head stock.

❖ To mount your turning blank, simply drill a hole at the center to slip over the mandrel. (Later, you will use the hole to assemble the project.)

❖ Clamp the blank against the mandrel fixture using the tailstock live center, and a block to protect the turning.

Friction drives the workpiece while the mandrel keeps it centered as shown in the drawings.

THREAD CADDY

Turn the blank to the diameter shown on the base template. Round over the edge of the base turning. Form the profile shown on the top (the side facing the lathe headstock). Sand the turning, and dismount it from the lathe.

Chuck the 5" disk the same way. Turn it to the dimensions shown on the drawing. The hole runs all the way through the spool table, so you can turn the top profile on the blank's tailstock side. Sand the completed turning.

Making the Pincushion Holder

❖ Band-saw a 4"-diameter blank from 1¼"-thick material.

❖ Drill a ⅜" hole through the center. Mount the blank as before.

❖ With the tailstock and clamping fixture in position, turn the pincushion holder outside profile.

❖ Turn the hollow on top of the pincushion holder. A cup shape about ⅜" deep is all you need. Undercut the center where shown by the line on the template.

❖ When it reaches about ½" diameter, dismount the turning and remove the waste with a hand chisel or gouge.

Turning the Finals & Center Support

Remove the mandrel fixture, and install a spur-drive center on the headstock. Remove the clamping fixture from the tailstock live center. Mount a 10" length of 1¼" square stock between centers and round it to 1".

Turn the finial and center support, following the dimensions shown in the drawings. You can turn both parts on the same piece of stock. Lay out the finial near the tailstock end. At the bottom of the finial's tenon, allow ³⁄₁₆" for a parting-tool cut. Then, lay out the center support, starting from the tip of the top tenon (the shorter one).

A SET OF SPOOLS—

Refer to the sidebar "Wooden Spools" in Project Number 18, on page 88. You can make another mandrel fixture to help you turn them quickly and easily.

❖ Construct the new drive fixture with a ⁵⁄₁₆"-diameter mandrel and ¾"-diameter face around the mandrel.

❖ Use the clamping fixture you made previously. (Turn the small end to ¾" for easier working.)

For this project saw only eight 1⅛" × 1⅛" × 1¼" blanks for the spools. Mark the center on one end of each blank by drawing diagonal lines. Drill a ⁵⁄₁₆" hole lengthwise through the center of each.

Chuck a blank, and turn it to 1" diameter. With the skew, form a flange at each end and turn the body to ⅞" diameter. Apply a clear finish. Wrap the spools with different-colored threads.

Turn both parts to shape with the skew and gouge, leaving a supporting tenon about ⅛" diameter at the top of the finial ball. Sand, then part in between the finial's tenon and the center support's top tenon, leaving about ⅛" of stock. Part in at the bottom of the center support's bottom tenon, again leaving about ⅛".

Remove the turning from the lathe, and saw the pieces apart with a fine-tooth backsaw. Cut the waste from the top of the finial and the bottom of the center support.

Making the Feet & Spool Pegs

Now, turn the three feet. Mount a piece of ¾" square scrap wood about 6" long between centers. Round it down to ½" and lay out the feet along its length. Shape the feet with the skew, and form the tenon on each with the parting tool.

For the spool pegs, cut eight 1⅛" lengths of ¼" walnut dowel. Sand one end of each round. You also could turn the pegs from scrap wood. Finish-sand all parts.

Putting It All Together

Drill the holes for the spool pegs where shown on the drawing. Glue the spool pegs into the holes. Glue the feet into their holes on the base.

Apply a clear finish to all parts, leaving unfinished the tenons on the center support and finial (see "Sanding Suggestions" and "Finishes" earlier, on pages 8, 9, and 10. Allow the parts to dry while you stuff the pincushion (see "The Pincushion" in Project No. 18, on page 87, for making the pincushion).

You can use a utility knife to slit the top center of the pincushion and an awl to open a hole through the stuffing. Push the finial tenon through the pincushion, and glue it into the hole in the pincushion holder.

Now, enlarge the spool table's center hole slightly to allow the table to spin freely on the center support. Insert the bottom tenon of the center support through the top of the spool table. Glue the tenon into the hole in the base, taking care not to glue or trap the spool table. Glue the pincushion assembly to the top tenon of the center support (C/A adhesive will work for this). Install the feet to complete the caddy!

21 PINWHEEL-SWIRL VESSEL

This vessel is lots of fun to make and looks more complicated and impressive than it is to create. This example of the pinwheel-swirl vessel was made from dressed dimensional wood that is called "one-by"—or "1×"—and is actually less than 1" thick. Nominal 1× lumber can be purchased at any lumber company or hardwood supplier. The particular dimensions for this project as drawn can be varied to fit wood that you have available. However this example has been made from 1×—also called "four-quarter by," or ¼ ×—9½"-wide butternut with macassar ebony finial, lid, and base.

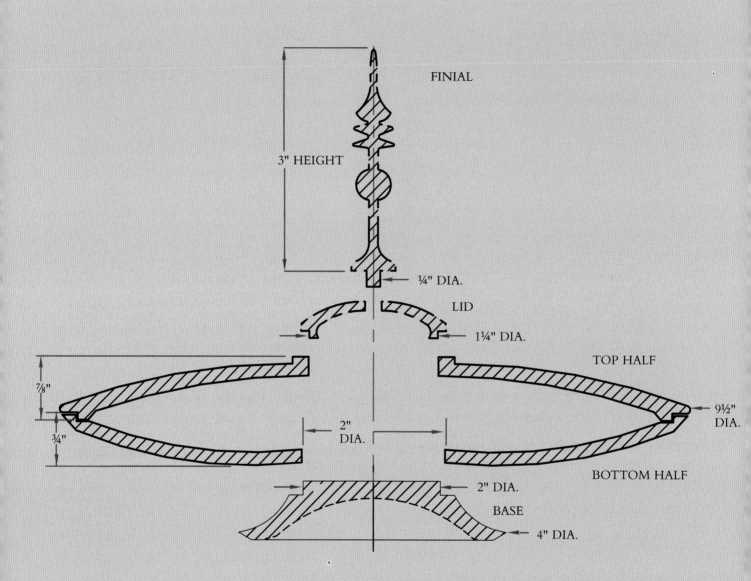

FINIAL

3" HEIGHT

¼" DIA.

LID

1¼" DIA.

TOP HALF

7/8"

9½" DIA.

¾"

2" DIA.

BOTTOM HALF

2" DIA.

BASE

4" DIA.

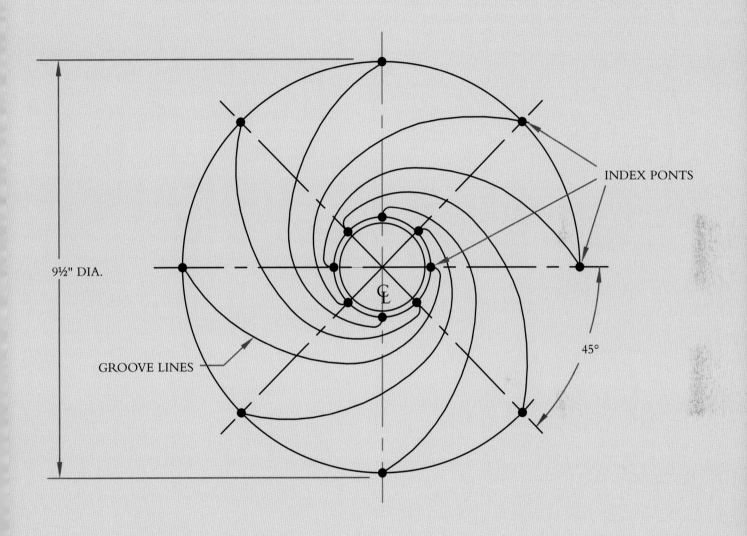

9½" DIA.

INDEX PONTS

45°

GROOVE LINES

Turning the Lid & Body Pieces

The lid, top half of the body, and bottom half of the body are turned on a screw chuck fitted with a ¼" threaded rod (see Project No. 10, "Using a Threaded-Rod Center," page 54).

❖ The two main body parts are then drilled to 2" with a Forstner bit. If you have a four-jaw chuck, you can drill first and expand the jaws to hold and turn these two pieces for the turning process.
❖ Use figure-eight calipers regularly to check wall thickness of the turnings. There is not a lot of wood to remove.

Turning the Base

❖ Make the base on a faceplate or on a faceplate with a waste block for gluing. Use the tailstock to hold it in place until it is turned and balanced.
❖ Turn the bottom of the base slightly concave so that it sits steadily. It adds to the quality of the turning to detail the bottom.

MAKING A TEMPLATE—

❖ Make an exact scale drawing on a thin piece of cardboard. (An empty cereal box works nicely.)
❖ Using a compass and a protractor, lay out the 45-degree lines.
❖ Starting on the opposite side of the opening, swing a line around and to the same point on the edge at 180 degrees.

A good drafting aid to use here is a plastic quarter-inch-square flexible line ruler that can be shaped to fit the surface and the curve desired.

Cut out a template of the segment from the cardboard drawing and, using the indexed points on the taped lid, mark the lines on the tape.

❖ Use skew lines and perhaps some chatter work to dress up the area where you will put your signature. This indicates pride in your work (and gives you a chance to "show off" a little).

Sand and finish all pieces before removing from the lathe (see "Sanding Suggestions" and "Finishes" earlier, on pages 8, 9, and 10).

Putting the Body Together

Glue the two body halves together. This will make it easier to control and handle the grooving process.

Surface Decoration

Cover the top with drafting tape so that lines can be drawn on the tape instead of the wood surface.

❖ Index the top into eight segments—360 degrees divided by 8 segments equals 45 degrees each segment. For each segment place a pencil mark at the bead near the lid and another at the outer edge of the piece.
❖ Use a template as described in the sidebar.
❖ Using the same process and equipment as described in Project No. 23, page 112, in "Carving the Shell Pattern," sand in the shallow grooves.

Groove the lid using a 1½"-to-2" rubber-backed sanding disk mounted in the headstock of the lathe using a Jacobs chuck. The quick-detach sanding disks are nice for this procedure. Be sure to run the sanding disk over the edge of the piece to break the line of the profile. The notch made by this sanding helps create the swirling impression of the project.

Turning the Finial

❖ The finial is turned between centers, using a small ⅜" spur center and a cup type live center.
❖ Turn the tenon to fit into the lid and with C/A glue fix in place.

The end product is delightful and does not reveal the simplicity with which it was made. Enjoy turning!

22

RINGS OF SATURN

It is still exciting to try new and different projects on the age-old lathe in this new age of space exploration. Looking at NASA photos, I was impressed with how Saturn's rings resembled the growth rings in a tree. This project is the result of an experiment done that same day, and can be completed easily in an afternoon.

Selecting the Wood

Choose a log that is as round as possible. Heart cracks can be a problem, but C/A glue works wonders to cure faults. Distinctive growth rings and sap wood of contrasting color can add to the visual effect. Experiment, because you can turn out some interesting patterns from any tree.

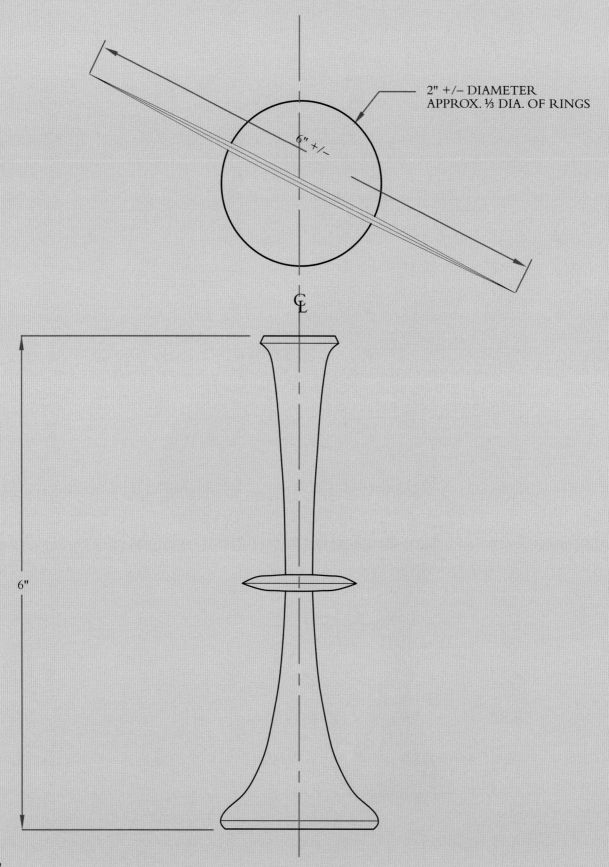

2" +/− DIAMETER
APPROX. ⅓ DIA. OF RINGS

6" +/−

C̶L

6"

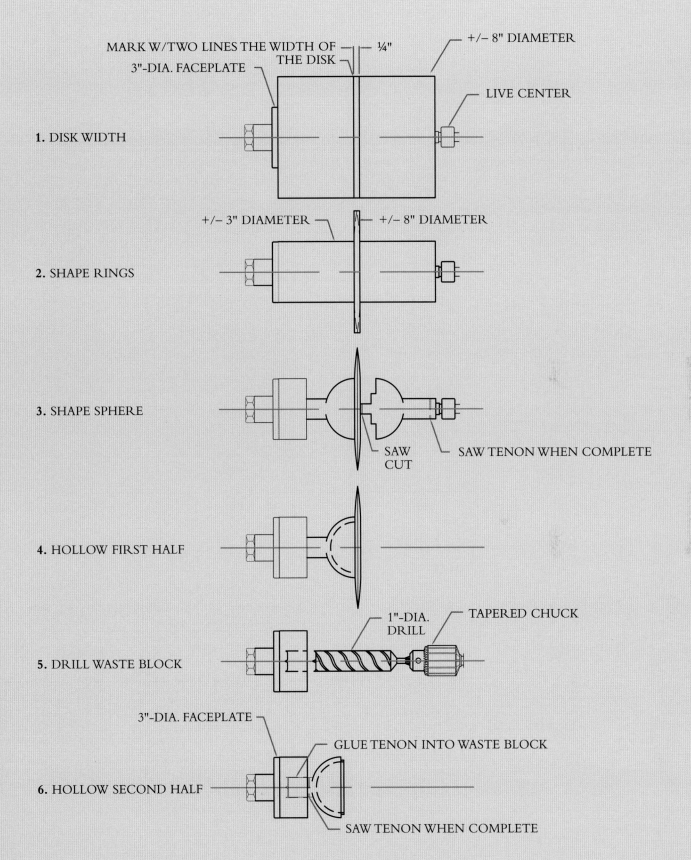

MARK W/TWO LINES THE WIDTH OF
THE DISK
¼"
+/− 8" DIAMETER
3"-DIA. FACEPLATE
LIVE CENTER

1. DISK WIDTH

+/− 3" DIAMETER
+/− 8" DIAMETER

2. SHAPE RINGS

3. SHAPE SPHERE

SAW
CUT
SAW TENON WHEN COMPLETE

4. HOLLOW FIRST HALF

1"-DIA.
DRILL
TAPERED CHUCK

5. DRILL WASTE BLOCK

3"-DIA. FACEPLATE

GLUE TENON INTO WASTE BLOCK

6. HOLLOW SECOND HALF

SAW TENON WHEN COMPLETE

Turning the Piece

❖ Attach the blank to the faceplate with sturdy screws, centering it as near as possible. I always support any turning with a live center in the tailstock until it is in the round.

As soon as the piece is turned into round, stop and mark the two lines that establish the width of the disk. In most woods, 3/16" wide is plenty for dressing and sanding. Should knots show in the disk, do not stop. They add to the effect; I call them "moon swirls."

❖ With a sharp parting tool, cut both sides of the disk down to what will become the outer diameter of the sphere.

The project looks balanced to me if the sphere is about one-third of the total diameter of the disk.

❖ Bring the body of the piece down to a uniform cylinder on each side of the disk.
❖ On the end next to the tailstock, turn a ½"-long tenon to the same diameter as one of your larger drill bits. In this case, I used a 1"-diameter brad point, but you can use any size that is convenient.

BALANCING THE SHAPE—

❖ Using outside calipers, measure the diameter of the cylinder. This dimension is not critical, but both sides of the sphere must match and a template makes it easy.
❖ Scribe a circle with the same diameter as the cylinder on a piece of light weight cardboard. With scissors or a sharp knife, cut out the template using the outer arc of the circle.
❖ Using the template as a gauge, turn the bottom of the sphere using a sharp chisel.

Remember, the sphere starts at the center of the disk, so shorten your template by ½ the thickness of the disk.

❖ Shape and prepare to part off that which will become the top of the sphere. Leave the outside tenon that will be used to hold and hollow the lid.

Also remember to start this hemisphere an additional 3/8" or so from the disk to allow for your parting cut and for an "inside" tenon that will fit into the disk.

❖ Using a parting tool, cut a lip on the lid that will be inserted into the disk later, then part off next to the disk. The waste stub outside the lid tenon will be used to center and support the lid for hollowing.
❖ Hollow out the sphere, making sure the lip on the lid fits snugly into the groove of the body at the disk.
❖ Sand and finish the body with the disk attached, before removing from the tenon.
❖ Back-saw the body from the tenon, leaving about 1/16" for sanding.

Remember, the sphere continues to be round into the tenon. If you saw it too close, the sphere will have a flat spot right where it will be noticed.

❖ With the drill chuck mounted in the tailstock, drill a hole in the waste block mounted on the faceplate. If your lathe does not have this capacity, turn a hole in the waste block to fit the lid tenon made earlier. Make sure the tenon fits tight, centered and running true. Use C/A glue to glue in the tenon.
❖ Hollow the lid as you would any bowl, making sure you leave the lip to fit the body.
❖ Saw off as before. I used a sanding pad in the drill chuck to hand sand the tenon off both pieces. Use a circular motion and you will find it easy to blend the shape of the sphere round as you remove the tenon.

Remember to spray with Deft™, so the glue will not show if you elect to glue the lid on permanently. I like to put something inside the sphere to prove it is hollow before I glue it up. Usually, I will use a couple of BB pellets from my grandson's air rifle.

Turning the Stand

Turn a stand for the piece between centers. This should be no taller than the total diameter of the disk. The bottom is concave so that it sits upright. The top should be about one-third the diameter of the sphere and hollowed slightly. You can use the template from before, and, in reverse, make the top of the stand fit the sphere. Apply your favorite finish to stand and project and you can tilt the "Rings of Saturn" to any angle you wish for better viewing.

23

SCALLOP-SHELL LIDDED BOX

Scallop shells are collected by anyone who has ever strolled along a beach. They catch our eye with their shape, form, and color. In this project, we use the grain pattern and color of the wood to create a scallop-shell lid.

Make It a Music Box

If you would like to, you can add an electronic battery-powered music mechanism that contains a light-sensitive switch that turns the music on when the box is opened and off when it is closed. Music-box mechanisms are available from many suppliers (see page 51).

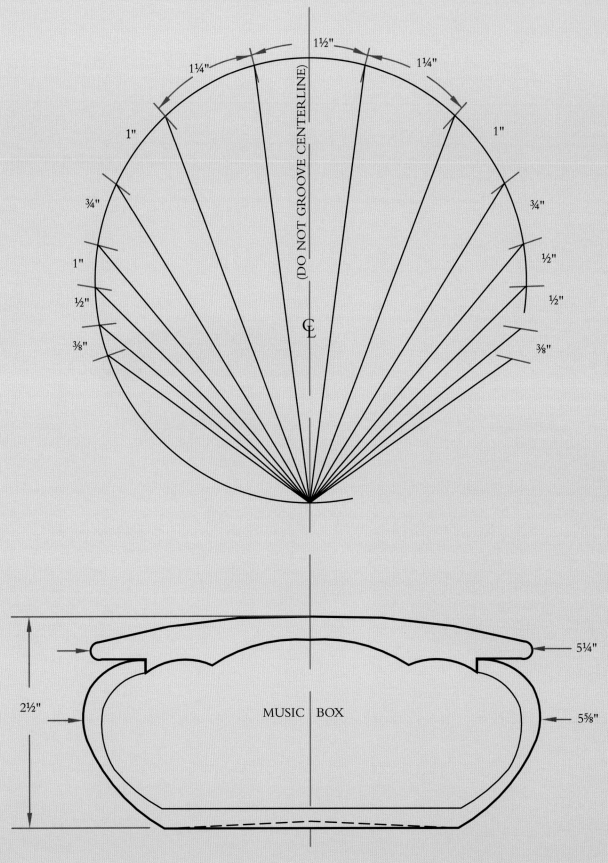

1½"

1¼"　　　　　　　　　1¼"

1"　　(DO NOT GROOVE CENTERLINE)　　　1"

¾"　　　　　　　　　　　　¾"

1"　　　　　　　　　　　½"

½"　　　　　　　　　　　½"

C_L

⅜"　　　　　　　　　　　⅜"

5¼"

2½"

MUSIC　BOX

5⅝"

Selecting the Wood

A good wood choice would be cocobolo, butternut, ash, maple, mesquite, or your favorite found wood. It should be quarter-sawed with an obvious grain pattern. Wood cut this way will have closer graining on the side that was nearer to the center of the log. This grain pattern is used to mimic the growth lines in the scallop shell, which are very close when young and get further apart the older it becomes. This same growth pattern occurs in a tree.

Turning the Pieces

❖ Start with a waste block in a chuck or screwed to a 3" faceplate. Bring up the tailstock with a cup-and-pin live center to secure the project.
❖ Turn to a balanced cylinder.
❖ With a parting tool make a straight-in cut about of the distance from the tailstock end.

It is more time-efficient to make the inside of the box lid first while you can use the body of the box as a jam chuck. It is not necessary to even measure the lip that will fit inside the box. Just make certain that it is small enough in diameter to give the box wall enough material for structural integrity when you turn it to fit.

Make sure that the tenon or lip that will be inserted into the body of the box is turned parallel to the axis and is long enough to make the lid fit securely when finished. Sand and apply finish before removing the attaching tenon with a backsaw.

❖ Reverse the lid and measure the connecting lip with calipers. Hollow out the body only enough to make a good tight fit for the lid of the box.

When the lid is press-fitted into the body, the outside of the top can then be turned, sanded, and finished while attached to the box.

Hollowing Out the Body

Put the finished lid aside and hollow out the body of the box. Drill a hole to serve as a depth guide; this is always a good practice when hollowing vessels. Do not sand or scrape against the surface that holds the lid. Use figure-eight calipers to determine if you have a consistent wall thickness.

MARQUETRY—

Should you desire to make an inlay in the lid instead of a scallop-shell design, it can easily be done at this stage.

❖ Make a disk out of a contrasting-color wood about one third the diameter of the lid and approximately ⅛" thick.
❖ With a parting tool take out the center of the lid to the depth and diameter of the disk. Glue the disk in place with C/A glue.
❖ Another, smaller disk can be made and inserted in the first to create an even more impressive box.

A suggestion for the second disk is to make it out of the same wood as the box. Use your creative imagination. Another turner used this idea and inserted a ring of PVC pipe that made an interesting white ring, like ivory, in the lid between the two color-contrasting wood inserts.

To detail the bottom, use a four-jaw chuck that will expand to fit the opening of the box. This setup will probably take a little adjusting to have the turning perfectly centered. Use a leather pad on a cup-and-pin live center in the tailstock to hold the box against the chuck until it can be tightened correctly. Be careful to not get the chuck too tight or you may split the box.

With the box bottom now accessible, you can turn it slightly concave so it will sit properly on a table. Also check the thickness—or perhaps I should say the thinness—of the bottom material. When sanding the bottom, do not over-sand or you can create enough heat to crack the thin bottom. Sanding creates friction and friction generates heat. Should you sand too long in the bottom, it will crack from heat expansion. Power sanding works well and saves time, but you must be aware of the circumstance. Regularly check the surface by feeling it with your fingertips. If it feels warm, give it a chance to cool before you continue.

111

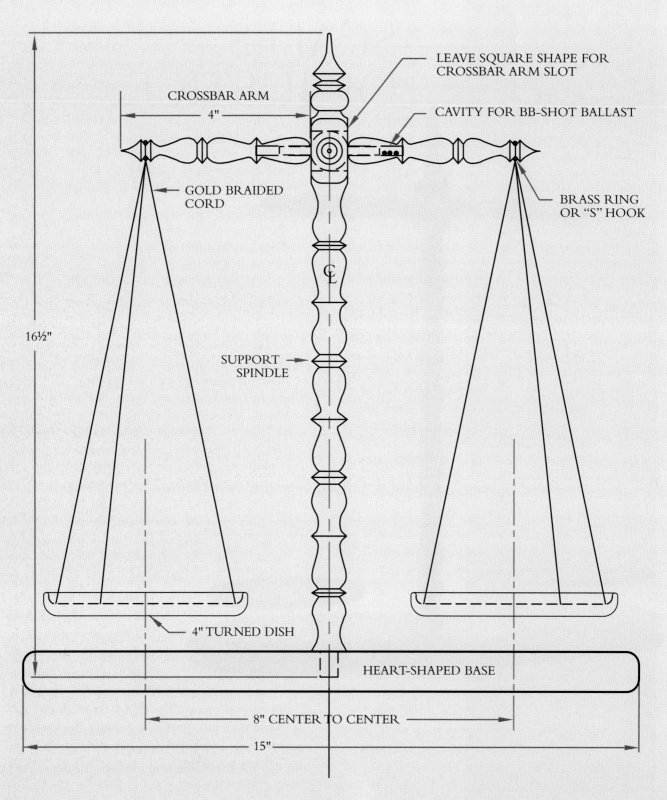

LEAVE SQUARE SHAPE FOR
CROSSBAR ARM SLOT

CAVITY FOR BB-SHOT BALLAST

CROSSBAR ARM

4"

GOLD BRAIDED
CORD

BRASS RING
OR "S" HOOK

C L

SUPPORT
SPINDLE

16½"

4" TURNED DISH

HEART-SHAPED BASE

8" CENTER TO CENTER

15"

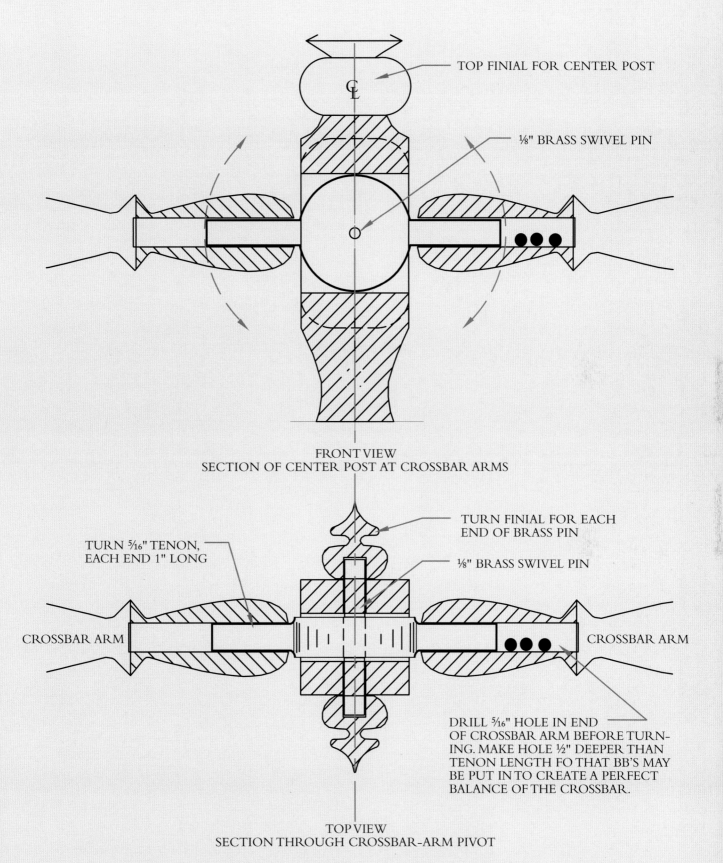

TOP FINIAL FOR CENTER POST

⅛" BRASS SWIVEL PIN

C L

FRONT VIEW
SECTION OF CENTER POST AT CROSSBAR ARMS

TURN FINIAL FOR EACH
END OF BRASS PIN

TURN ⁵⁄₁₆" TENON,
EACH END 1" LONG

⅛" BRASS SWIVEL PIN

CROSSBAR ARM

CROSSBAR ARM

DRILL ⁵⁄₁₆" HOLE IN END
OF CROSSBAR ARM BEFORE TURN-
ING. MAKE HOLE ½" DEEPER THAN
TENON LENGTH FO THAT BB'S MAY
BE PUT IN TO CREATE A PERFECT
BALANCE OF THE CROSSBAR.

TOP VIEW
SECTION THROUGH CROSSBAR-ARM PIVOT

115

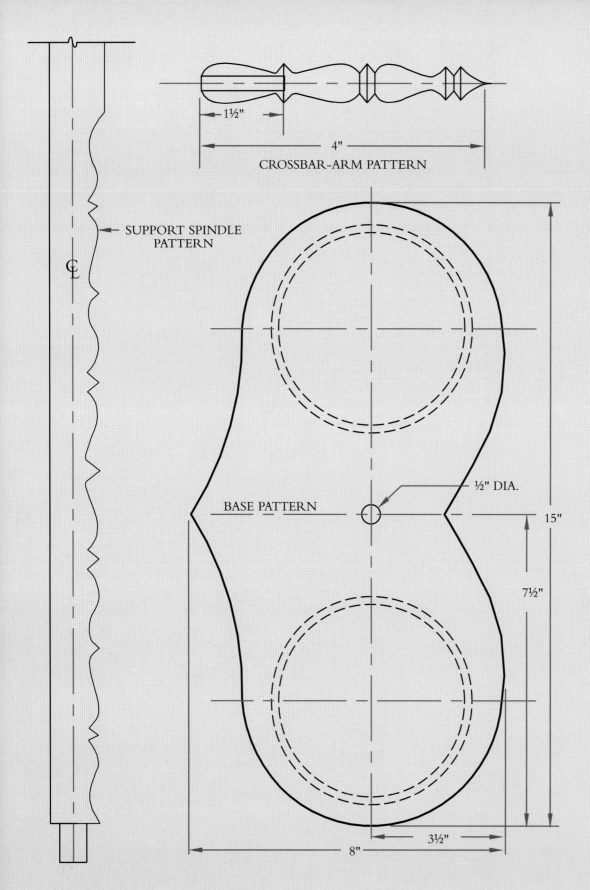

CROSSBAR-ARM PATTERN

1½"

4"

SUPPORT SPINDLE
PATTERN

C̶L̶

½" DIA.

BASE PATTERN

15"

7½"

3½"

8"

Preparing the Pans

Turn the two pans from one piece that is ¾" thick, 4" in diameter split on the band saw. I band-sawed the circles and mounted them on a waste block attached to a 2½"-diameter faceplate with double-stick carpet tape. The compass point indent served as a centering reference for the live center.

❖ I held the mounted blank in place with a small dowel on the cup-and-pin live center. A small pad of leather glued to the dowel kept the setup from making a deeper indentation.

❖ The pans were turned, and detailed with a Bonnie Klein™ chatter tool (available from Klein Design, Inc., 17910 SE 110th St., Renton, WA 98059, 425-226-5937, www.bonnieklein.com, bonnie@bonnie klein.com). This gives the rather plain wood some decoration. Both top and bottom were decorated with skew lines and chatter marks (see sidebar).

Turning the Spindle and Crossbars

The vertical spindle is a rather straight exercise in skew work using any pattern that you wish. Leave a flat area to drill the crossbars. Turn a tenon on the end to be inserted into the base. I used a ½"-diameter tenon ½" long. I did not want the tenon to extend through the ¾"-thick base so a Forstner bit was used to drill a nice flat bottomed hole stopping short of going through.

The crossbars are a fun part of the project, made in three pieces. One center piece is turned between centers with a long tenon on each end. The middle is left flat to insert through the vertical support. I started with a ⅜"-thick piece, 1" wide × 4" long.

❖ Turn a 1"-long, 5⁄16"-diameter tenon on each end. These tenons will be inserted into holes drilled in the spindle end of the crossbar arms.

❖ A ⅛"-diameter pivot hole is centered and drilled to let the arm move when completed. I used a ⅛" brass rod (available at local hobby shops) as the pivot pin.

Cut the brass rod for the pivot pin about ¼" longer than the squared area of the support spindle. Turn two small finials to go over the ends to hide the rod.

❖ To make the small finials, drill ⅛" holes ⅛" deep in two ½"-square blocks. Use a small piece of the brass rod as a mandrel held in the Jacobs chuck for

CHATTER WORK—

❖ Outline the area in which you wish to do the decoration with a skew-point mark.

❖ With the lathe running at medium speed, start at the smallest diameter and pull the chatter tool across the outlined area.

Stop carefully at the largest-diameter skew line. Make only one pass. Additional passes only make the pattern less visible and you wind up with a mess.

turning the finials.

❖ To turn the two crossbar arms, first drill a 5⁄16" hole 1½" deep in two pieces of 5"-long, ¾"-square stock.

❖ Use a ½" spur center on one end and a small cone live center inserted into the 5⁄16" hole to center and support the blank.

The purpose for the hole being drilled ½" deeper than the length of the tenon that will be inserted is that this arm must be balanced. The extra cavity can be used to insert a few BB's.

Making the Base

The heart-shaped base is wide enough to let the pans come to rest. Design your own base. The pans can come to rest on the tabletop if you like, if the support of the base is steady enough.

I used some gold braided cord to make the suspension cords. A drop of C/A glue works well and looks better than a knot to secure the cord to the weighing pans. I made two "S" hooks from small brass rods to hook the pans to the crossbar arms.

Finishing

To finish the project, I used two coats of clear satin Deft™ and buffed the pieces with the Beall™ Buffing System. (See "Sanding Suggestions" and "Finishes" earlier, on pages 8, 9, and 10.)

With the scale done, turn some small "weights" to go in the weighing pans just for show. These may be turned of the same wood or a contrasting-color wood.

25 CARVED-EDGE PLATTER

This project involves turning a thin platter, indexing and caving the edge to create a showpiece from highly figured wood. Occasionally, we all find a large piece of crotch wood or highly figured stress wood that has only a thin area of figure. This project is a good one for utilizing that thin area of figure to make a prized piece.

Cut the blank with a chain saw into a slab no more than 1" thick. Check the figuring by running it through a planer, using a handheld power planer, or running a belt sander over it. Try to keep the thickness as consistent as possible.

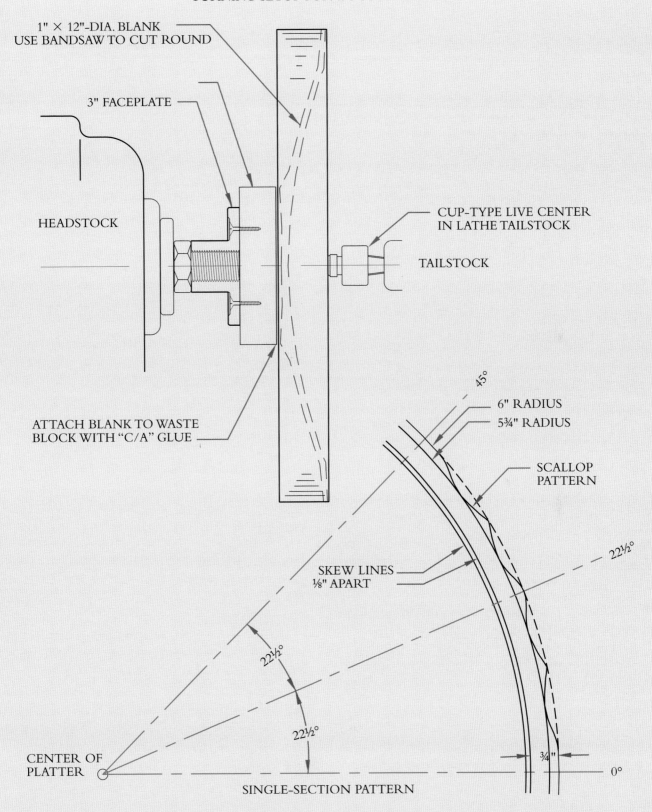

TURNING SETUP FOR WOODEN PLATTER

1" × 12"-DIA. BLANK
USE BANDSAW TO CUT ROUND

3" FACEPLATE

HEADSTOCK

CUP-TYPE LIVE CENTER
IN LATHE TAILSTOCK

TAILSTOCK

ATTACH BLANK TO WASTE
BLOCK WITH "C/A" GLUE

45°

6" RADIUS
5¾" RADIUS

SCALLOP
PATTERN

22½°

SKEW LINES
⅛" APART

22½°

22½°

CENTER OF
PLATTER

¾"

0°

SINGLE-SECTION PATTERN

Turning the Platter

Once the best area of figure is identified, decide which will be top and bottom. The top will be the side shown most so let the best figuring be for the top.

❖ Scribe a circle as large as possible to utilize the wood. Band-saw out the blank. Keep in mind the size capacity of your lathe. In this example, 12 inches was as large as the lathe would permit.

❖ Using a 3" faceplate with a waste block, use C/A glue to secure the blank to the waste block. A series of concentric circles drawn with a compass will help you center the piece.

Bring up the tailstock with a cup-type live center to hold the turning blank against the waste block. If you have a cup-and-pin center, remove the pin as it will leave a hole that cannot be sanded away.

TURNING AT LOW SPEED—

The lathe should run at a slow speed. If you have a variable-speed lathe, do not try to increase the speed after it is in balance. The surface-edge speed of a 12" diameter is very fast and any imbalance or imperfection in the wood can be hazardous. You must wear a protective face shield when working on a piece of this diameter. Do not stand in line with the turning piece in case a hidden crack develops and throws a piece across the shop. Keep safety in mind.

❖ Turn both back and front from this same setup. Most tool rests will allow you to turn the back side. Use a deep-Vee bowl gouge in ½" or ⅝" size. Check the thickness regularly with a figure-eight caliper.

Good wood without flaws can be turned to ³⁄₁₆" thickness. A platter should be uniform in thickness except for the bead that makes the base.

Use two skew lines about ⅛" apart in ¾" from the edge. This will act as a frame for separating the carved area from the rest of the surface.

❖ Sand the surfaces, other than under the waste block and tailstock (see "Sanding Suggestions" and "Finishes" earlier, on pages 8, 9, and 10).

❖ Apply a single coat of finish so that the tape you will put over the carved area will not leave residue on the raw wood.

Carving the Edge

Cover the area to be carved with drafting tape. Drafting tape is available at office supply stores and does not transfer the adhesive as much as masking tape.

❖ Index the area to be carved into eight segments— 360 degrees divided by 8 equals 45 degrees each. Then divide those sections in half (22½ degrees) to establish a centerline in each segment.

❖ Holding a pencil on the tool rest against the tape, slowly rotate the piece by hand and make a line ¼" in from the edge of the piece. This will indicate the depth of the pattern to be carved (see the drawing).

Make a template for one section out of lightweight cardboard. An empty cereal box works nicely. Using the index lines on the tape for guides, draw the pattern for each section on the tape.

❖ Use a burr on a high-speed handheld grinder to shape the edge through the tape. This will work quickly, so be careful to not make an undercut. Remember, "Stay within the lines."

❖ Use a split mandrel with small pieces of sandpaper mounted in the same rotary tool to sand the edges. Remember to wear eye and lung protection.

Final Sanding

When finished carving, remove the piece from the waste block with rocking motion or bump of the hand to break the bond of the glue.

The area supported by the tailstock and waste block can now be sanded. Use a 3" or 4" sanding pad mounted in a Jacobs chuck in the headstock. Holding the turning in your hand to guide the piece, be careful not to sand a low spot in the surface.

Handsand the entire surface with your final grit to remove any scratches left from earlier.

The project turns an otherwise unusable piece of wood into a thing of beauty.

26

CANDLEHOLDER WITH CARVED-THROUGH CHIMNEY

This project involves a little ingenuity, some basic turning skills, and having fun with the indexing exercise.

A large cypress knee had been gathering dust in the corner of my shop for some time. I was saving it for the right moment, but I didn't know what it might become or how the wood itself would respond to turning.

I became aware of a contest to turn a candleholder, and that was all I needed; this odd piece of cypress knee was what I had at hand and so it became the project wood by default. Out of curiosity, I decided to see how the cypress knee would turn. The wood was lightweight, fairly soft, and had some interesting graining.

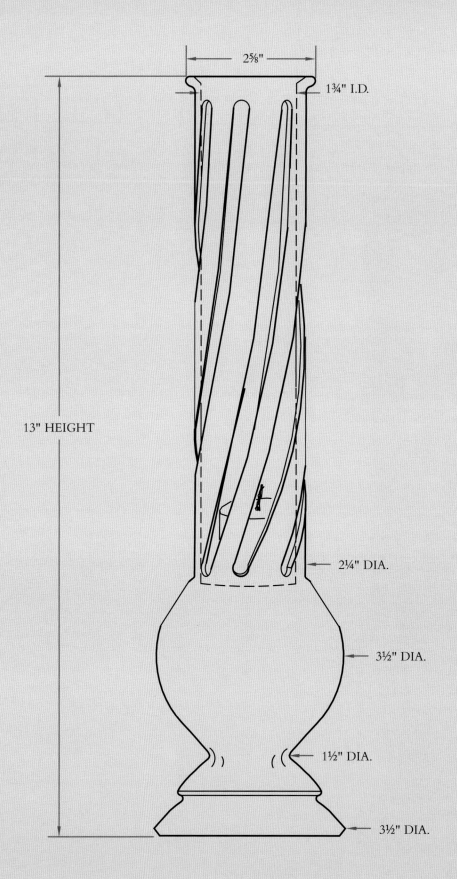

2⅝"

1¾" I.D.

13" HEIGHT

2¼" DIA.

3½" DIA.

1½" DIA.

3½" DIA.

Preparing the Piece for Turning

❖ With heavy screws, the piece of cypress was mounted on a 3" faceplate.

❖ With the tailstock in place, it was turned to a balanced cylinder about 3½" in diameter by 13" long outside the screws in the faceplate.

❖ Using the Jacobs chuck in the tailstock, a 1¾" hole was bored 8½" deep with a Forstner bit.

Because the shank on the bit was too short to go that deep, an 8" No. 2 Morse taper extension was used. Frequent retraction of the bit for cleaning is imperative to keep from binding up the bit and splitting the wood.

Note that turning supplies such as the No. 2 Morse taper or a Jacobs chuck are available from many sources including Craft Supplies USA (see page 26), Woodcraft Supply and Cutting Edge Woodworkers Supply (see page 112), Packard Woodworks, 215 South Trade St., Tryon, NC 28782, 800-683-8876, www.packardwoodworks.com, packard@alltel.net.

Shaping the Piece

❖ Remove the chuck and extension from the tailstock and insert a cone type live center in the hole.

❖ Turn the base and body shape first.

❖ Then turn the chimney area down to a consistent ⅛" wall thickness 2" in diameter.

❖ Sand and finish the outside (see "Sanding Suggestions" and "Finishes" earlier, on pages 8, 9, 10).

Cover the area to be cut through with masking tape so that you can use a pencil to draw on the tape instead of the wood.

Indexing the Cylinder

❖ Index the cylinder into eight sections—360 degrees divided by 8 equal 45 degrees each section.

❖ Mark a point at each end of the cylinder at the same index stop.

❖ To achieve the spiral, lay a flexible ruler from one point to the third point at the opposite end around the cylinder and continue around to the point of beginning. Each line will rotate 90 degrees around the axis.

❖ Drill a ⅜" hole at each point of index at both ends of the chimney.

❖ With the flexible ruler draw parallel lines ⅜" apart from hole to hole as in the spiral layout above each, rotating 90 degrees around the axis.

Make the Base Concave

Before cutting the slots, it is best to turn the base concave and remove the turning from the lathe. This always helps to ensure that the finished piece will sit steadily on a tabletop or other flat surface.

Carving the Spiral Slots

❖ With a ¼" router bit in the drill press and the turning nestled in a plastic bag of wood chips, slowly rotate the turning to follow between the lines to cut a spiral slot.

❖ The bag of chips allows you to rotate and feed the turning at the same time.

Certainly there are many other methods of cutting the spiral slots, but this worked well. It does require hand-carving and sanding to get the lines straight.

USE CAUTION—

❖ Once the slots are cut, do not turn the lathe on until you have re-taped around the chimney.

❖ Be careful and always use caution: The wood between the slots is too thin and centrifugal force will break the piece if the lathe is turned on without protection.

When the piece is finished, the chimney will have a "see-through" basket-weave appearance. This design won the contest that was my incentive to use the cypress knee. Perhaps you will produce a winner also.

It will hold a candle, but setting fire to the wick would only be done by the turner. Perhaps a very small candle—for a very short period. No, just forget lighting the candle; this is just for looks!

27

HOLLOW FLASK

Many times I have looked around the shop for a nice, solid turning blank and found only dimensional lumber that had been cut and planed into pieces that seemed as if they would be too thin to be used for turning.

One of the delightful things about making this lovely hollow flask is that this project will let you utilize some of that beautifully figured wood that was not thick enough to turn. You can lay out the entire project on a small board to create a nice turning with very little waste.

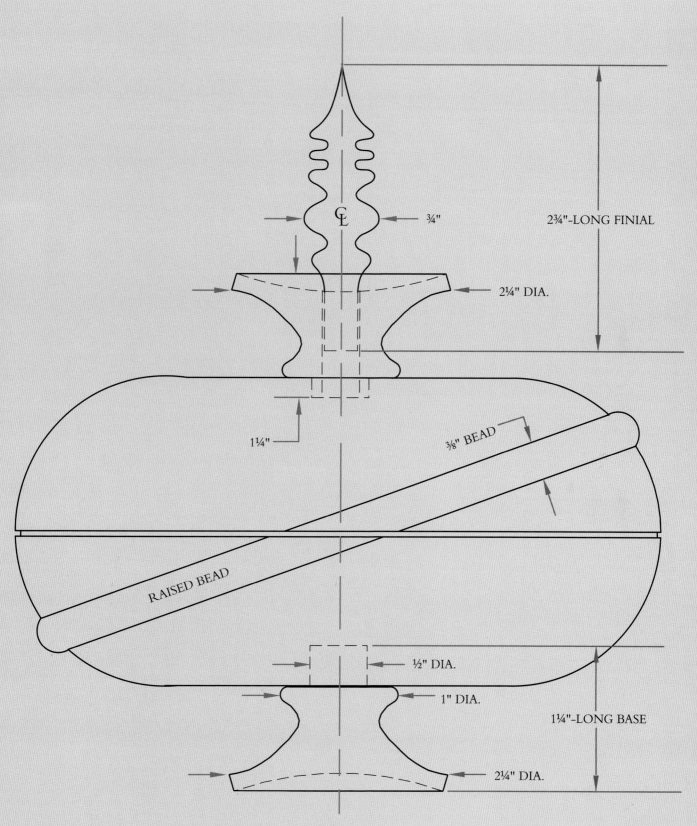

C
L

¾"

2¾"-LONG FINIAL

2¼" DIA.

1¼"

⅜" BEAD

RAISED BEAD

½" DIA.

1" DIA.

1¼"-LONG BASE

2¼" DIA.

125

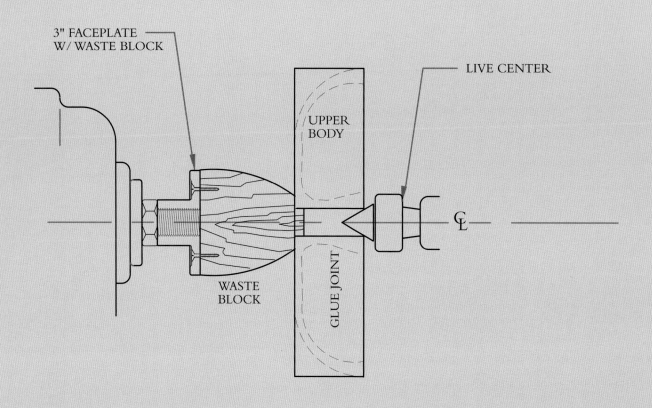

3" FACEPLATE
W/ WASTE BLOCK

UPPER
BODY

LIVE CENTER

WASTE
BLOCK

GLUE JOINT

C L

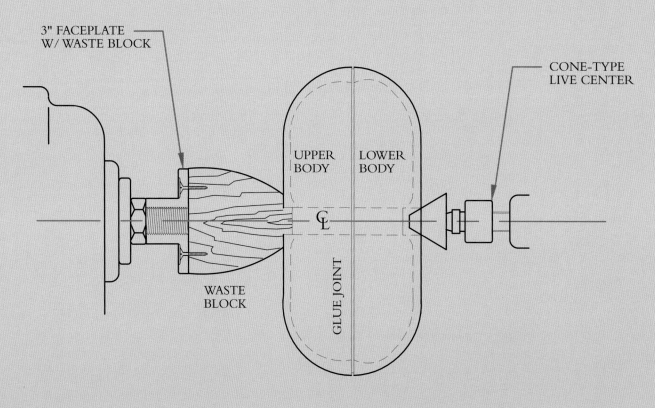

3" FACEPLATE
W/ WASTE BLOCK

CONE-TYPE
LIVE CENTER

UPPER
BODY

LOWER
BODY

C L

WASTE
BLOCK

GLUE JOINT

126

Laying Out the Project

Lay out your project using a compass (see drawings). Mark the tops of all pieces which will become the body of the turning. By folding the two main body pieces so that the bottoms become the joined surfaces, you can rotate the pieces and achieve a butterfly grain match.

❖ Drill a hole in both the upper body and lower body to accommodate the base and top. On larger pieces use ⅞"-to-1" bits. On smaller projects adjust the hole and tenon size down to reduce the weight.

❖ Using a waste block on a 3" faceplate, prepare a tenon to fit the hole drilled in the body.

Remember to check the marks made earlier on the turning blank to indicate the orientation of the grain.

Turning

Place the blank on the tenon and secure in place with a large point live center. I use a "one-way"-cone live center system that offers quality and versatility.

❖ Turn the corners off to produce the desired shape for the outside of the vessel.

I used a deep-fluted bowl gouge, followed with a French-ground wide shear scraper that I call my "eraser," to minimize sanding time. The bowl gouge will also let you excavate the inside to the desired wall thickness. This procedure is similar to turning an open bowl.

❖ Check often with a figure-eight caliper to keep from getting it too thin in spots. A good consistent wall thickness is necessary for stability.

❖ After hollowing remove from the waste-block chuck and, using a bench chisel, remove the inside tenon.

One nice part about this design is that we do not have to sand and finish the inside. (I like Dale Nish's comment that "If they can't feel or see inside, you can tell them you sanded to 600-grit and no one will know.")

Gluing

With both upper and lower body turned, check grain alignment and place glue on both flanges. Place back on the same chuck and, using the tailstock as a clamp, press the two halves together. Be careful not to exert too much pressure or you will crack the pieces.

If you use C/A glue to glue the two pieces together, you can go back to turning right away. There are always some minor misalignments in the two halves, plus the excess glue to turn off. With a shear scraping cut, true up the glued joint with light cuts.

HOLLOW TIME CAPSULE—

Should you want to prove that it is hollow, before you glue the pieces together, place a new coin inside with the current year's date. Since it cannot come out, it makes for an interesting bit of conversation and in a few generations may become more valuable than the turning—who knows!

If you would like to carry the project further, leave the wall thickness about 5⁄16" thick. With a strip of ⅜"-wide masking tape, place an elliptical ring around the body. Now, with a 1½"-to-2" sanding disc placed in the head stock using a three jaw drill chuck, sand a groove up to the masking tape and taper to the radius. Start with 150-grit and go up. At 220-grit, remove the tape and blend the beaded edges into the surface, creating an elliptical bead around the piece.

Turning the Top, Base & Finial

The top can be turned on the same chuck by reducing the size of the tenon and using the same procedure.

The base and finial are spindle-turning projects. Use calipers for accuracy and fit. The base should fit snugly before being glued and the finial should fit like a cork with a slight taper.

I finish all pieces as they are completed (see "Sanding Suggestions" and "Finishing" earlier, on pages 8, 9, and 10). When all pieces are finished, assemble. Be very careful with excess glue!

Once it is assembled, I buff the project with a three-buff system using Tripoli™, White Diamond™, and carnauba wax, in that order, on 9" muslin wheels.

Now you can sign, date, and identify the wood on the bottom and wait for the coin to gain value.

28 HANDLED URN

I have found it to be a lot of fun to turn a tall, hollow vessel and install carved handles to create a different look. It gives a sense of lightness and fragility.

Selecting the Wood

Overall you need to start with a single piece of 4" × 4" wood that is at least 18" long. Choose a beautiful piece of quality hardwood so that the finished urn will be as attractuive as it can be. For the body and lid you will need one piece that is 4" × 4" × 10". For the handles you will need an additional 8" piece of the same wood.

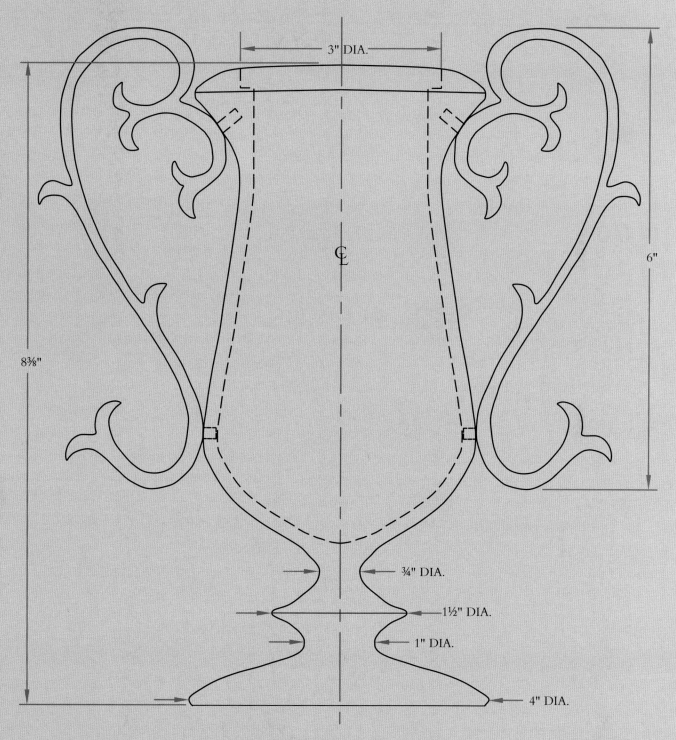

3" DIA.

6"

C̶L

8⅜"

¾" DIA.

1½" DIA.

1" DIA.

4" DIA.

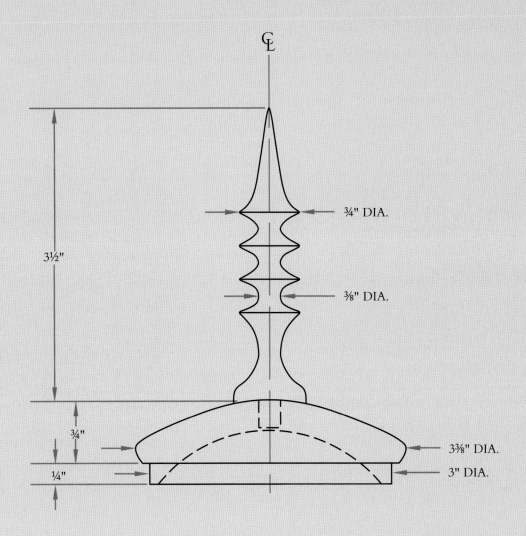

℄

3½"

¾" DIA.

⅜" DIA.

¾"

¼"

3⅜" DIA.

3" DIA.

LID WITH FINIAL

130

Turning the Body & Lid

❖ Attach the 10"-long piece to a 3" faceplate and turn to round. Always use the tailstock to secure the piece between centers when you can.
❖ Part off a ¾"-thick piece for the top. This will allow the grain in the top to match the body.
❖ Drill a ½" hole 6" deep in the body piece to act as a depth guide, and excavate the inside of the turning.

When you have reached the bottom of the drill hole, your depth will be correct. Rough in the outside of the body and check wall thickness regularly with a figure-eight caliper. Do not reduce the size of the foot until the major part of the body is turned and sanded. With a parting tool, make the joint for the lid.

Put a cone-type live center on the tailstock and bring up to snug fit into the opening. Do not force the cone into the opening or you can crack the wood. Use only enough pressure to stabilize the turning.

❖ Using a spindle gouge, turn the foot and make a bead on the stem. Beads on stems look nice, add structural integrity, and reduce distortion, all of which are good design features.
❖ Use a sharp parting tool to reduce the size of the wood between the foot and the faceplate screws to about ½" diameter. Make this cut slightly concave.

Remove the piece from the lathe before sawing off the tenon that attaches it to the faceplate. A bench chisel and a small amount of sanding will finish the bottom.

To detail the bottom, the waste block can be turned to fit the opening in the top of the piece. With a cup-type live center, the sawed tenon can be used to rechuck the piece to still turn true. Chatter work and a few skew lines will dress up the bottom of the pieces.

❖ Now take the ¾" piece that was saved for the top and drill a ¼" hole in the center.
❖ Using a screw center, turn the bottom of the lid to fit in the top of the urn as you would in any lidded box. Detail the inside of the lid if you wish.

Turning the Finial

❖ Between centers, turn a 1¼" × 4" finial.
❖ Cut a ¼"-diameter tenon long enough to go through the lid on one end.

To create the deep coves, I used a chisel ground down to a ⅛" roundnose. When making the beads on the finial, you should keep in mind the shape of the bead above the foot.

MAKING THE HANDLES—

Draw a few different designs freehand on a piece of paper taped next to the body pattern until you find one you prefer.

Handles about two-thirds as long as the body give a proportion that I like. It goes back to the "one-third–two-thirds" rule (see page 26).

❖ Make a pattern. Cereal and cracker boxes work very well for cardboard templates. To draw parallel lines, tape two pencils together with a spacer in between.
❖ Scroll-saw out the handles, being careful not to cut off the mounting tenons.
❖ To reduce the possibility of the tenon's breaking off later, drill and glue in a small brass pin.

Brass rods in various sizes can be purchased at most craft shops in 12" lengths. To speed up the carving process, I use a variable-speed, reversible mini-grinder to both round and sand. A split mandrel, available from most woodworking supply stores, makes an excellent flap sander.

❖ Be sure to wear a good dust mask and eye protection. The fine grains of grit that come off the rotating sandpaper can create a serious hazard for unprotected eyes.

Use a strip of drafting tape on each side of the body of the vessel to index and mark the drill holes for the handle tenons. I have found that it is easier to get the angles correct by drilling the holes to mount the handles with a handheld drill. Choose your grain direction carefully to put the best grain pattern forward.

Every project should end with a signature and a smile.

29 MASHRABEYA VESSEL

The traditional Egyptian turned-wood panels, called *mashrabeya,* caught my eye on a visit there. I asked several Egyptian master turners if they could incorporate the mashrabeya technique into a vessel form. I was told that it would be very complex. It thus became a challenge for me upon returning home. I discovered they were right! Complex, but not impossible.

I explored several designs, finally arriving back at a simple vessel in several parts that accommodated flat stock. To add a music box to the base, the finial was extended through the center, the winding key was ground off and inserted in a hole in the bottom of the finial shaft to allow the shaft to screw onto the threaded music-box winding shaft.

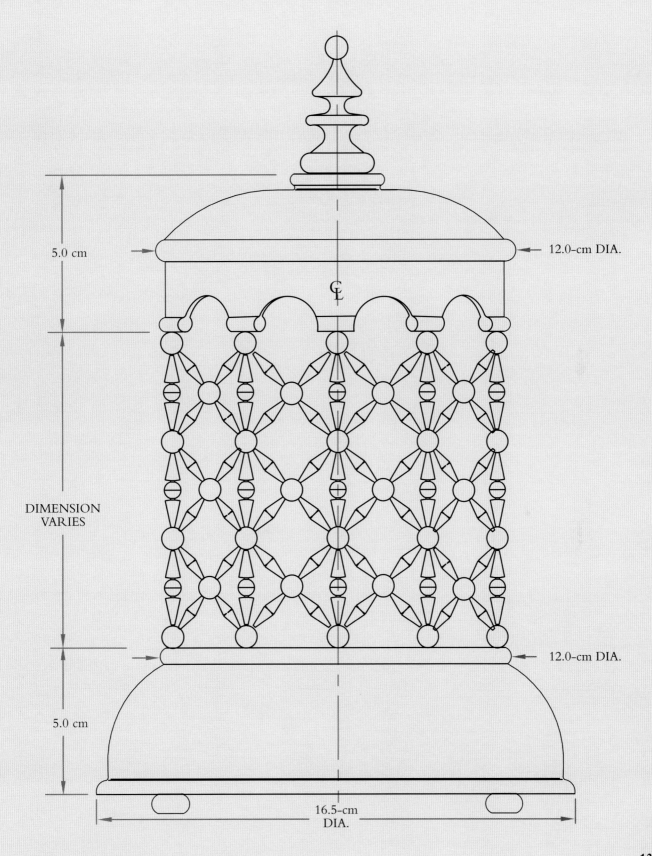

5.0 cm

12.0-cm DIA.

C̸L

DIMENSION
VARIES

12.0-cm DIA.

5.0 cm

16.5-cm
DIA.

133

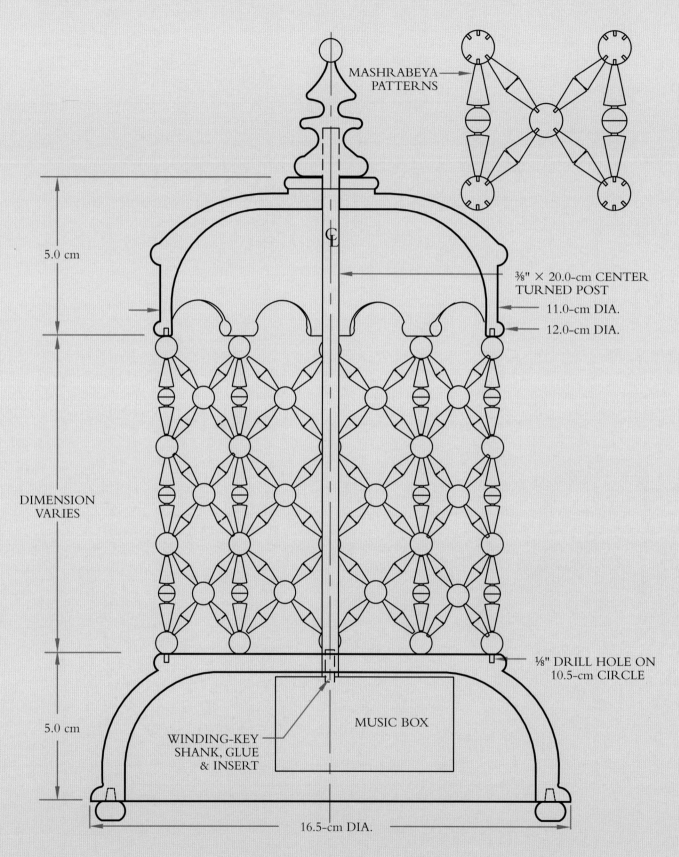

MASHRABEYA
PATTERNS

5.0 cm

C
L

⅜" × 20.0-cm CENTER
TURNED POST

11.0-cm DIA.

12.0-cm DIA.

DIMENSION
VARIES

⅛" DRILL HOLE ON
10.5-cm CIRCLE

5.0 cm

MUSIC BOX

WINDING-KEY
SHANK, GLUE
& INSERT

16.5-cm DIA.

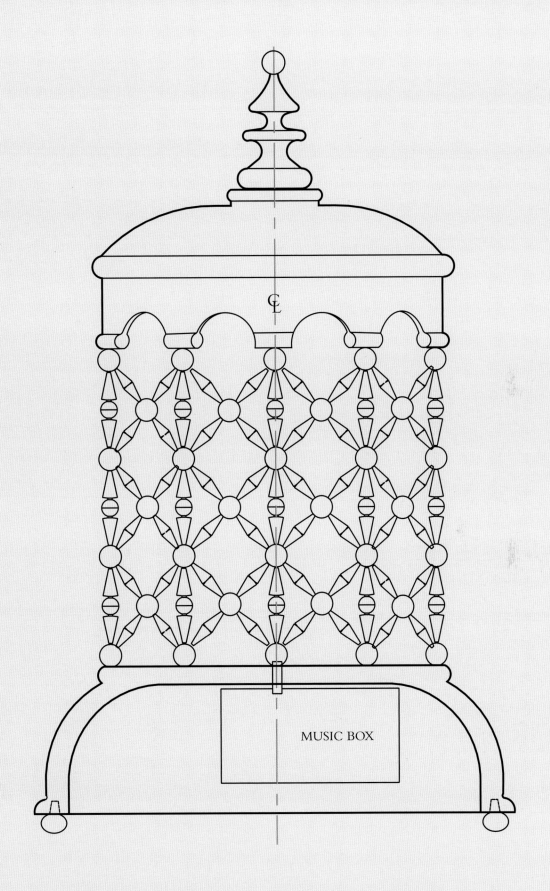

MUSIC BOX

SHARING SKILLS—

I had agreed to do my fifth volunteer project with the International Executive Service Corps overseas in Cairo, Egypt. I've enjoyed the travel as well as teaching other woodworkers in developing countries some of our techniques.

In what are called developing countries, an apprenticeship system is still in place and the links of that skill chain have not been broken. When our apprentice system in the United States was abandoned in the early part of this century, a silent tragedy began to evolve. The skills of master craftsmen were no longer passed on from generation to generation. Tools were lost, too, because in many cases the master had been a father or grandfather who would bequeath his shop with his craft. Most important, the love for and pride in work well done was no longer acquired through practice at the side of one whose life was his craft.

Perhaps the success of the American Association of Woodturners (see page 27) can be traced to a desire to acquire and pass along nearly lost ancient skills. I believe we have much to learn from those "underdeveloped" areas we sometimes still mistakenly regard as primitive.

My four previous volunteer projects had been in warm climates during our winter months. That worked out great! This time it was the Egyptian desert in July and August. Since Cairo is also 31 degrees north latitude I assumed the climate would be similar to our Texas summers. It was that and more. Daily temperatures were above 40 degrees C (105 degrees F); on one occasion in a summer sandstorm, it exceeded 52 degrees C (125 degrees F).

Indexing the Design

Once I had chosen the vessel design, work proceeded quickly up to indexing, where I had to determine the spindle design. You have to know the shape and size of the mashrabeya spindles before you can index and drill. To do this, I made an exact scale drawing of both the top and front view of the spindle layout.

I tried dividing my 5"-diameter vessel into ten and twelve segments. By making actual-scale drawings, you can see what the finished pattern will be. I thus selected the pattern of ten segments. The few moments spent at the drawing table probably saved several hours of turning, a tad of frustration, and more than a smidgen of my already strained religion.

This particular pattern would require a total of ten segments—36 degrees each segment. Each segment contains eleven spindles, for a total of 110 spindles, not including the seven turnings that make up the body of the vessel. This was going to be a wonderful challenge of turning skills!

Turning the Spindles

Faced with the duplication of so many spindles, I resorted to using a scratch block with wire nails located at the strategic points to mark the cylinders. I sized the cylinder diameters by using a standard ⅜" open-end wrench. This makes a great spanner gauge because it does not flex and even burnishes the wood as you slide it along the length of the cylinder.

For the tenon on each end of each spindle, I made another spanner gauge by drilling a ⅛" hole in a piece of metal and opening up the end with a file. Although the gauges and spanners take time to make, that too is fun and pays great dividends in quality control and ease of duplication.

I used a set of Klein Design™ Henry Taylor miniature chisels available from many suppliers (see pages 112, 117, and 123). The ¹⁄₁₆" parting tool and the ³⁄₁₆" spindle gouge worked best for beads. The grooves yielded to a shop-made tool made from a concrete nail. I sharpened the tip like that of an awl and flattened the top with a file. It worked nicely and did not try to run off the mark.

Assembling the Spindles

The traditional Egyptian panels do not contain glue or nails but are held together by the frame in which the individual elements are placed. In this project, assembly required the frugal use of C/A glue. Just imagine what the ancient Egyptians could have made if they had invented this glue.

Assembling the spindles, I tried several approaches. First, building a jig to assist in drilling the holes at the correct angle while allowing for just enough discrepancy to make assembly possible proved to be beyond my tolerance. I remembered watching while one of the Egyptian workers drilled the holes freehand. When I commented on his skill he said, "You have to learn to drill by hand—it is the only way." He was right! If the holes are clean and straight, as you would think best, there is no flex to allow for the assembly process. The holes must be slightly loose at the outer edge. You must "wallow out" the top of the hole by swinging the drill in an arc or by wobbling the piece.

I found it uncomfortable to be running a high-speed drill bit toward a part of my hand. I drilled the first few with the drawing underneath to line up the proper angle. After that, I found it quite easy to maintain the right angle. I drilled only one hole in the tip of my index finger.

For assembly, I reverted to the process used by the Egyptian experts, who use small pieces of string to hold the subassemblies together until they can be joined with those previously assembled. Additional string holds the subassemblies to each other until the whole complex has enough integrity to slip into the framing members. I found that dental floss worked best. Once the pieces are assembled, some quiet time using a small pair of scissors to remove all those little pieces of string only adds to the savor of the creative process.

Finishing

See "Sanding Suggestions" and "Finishes" earlier, on pages 8, 9, and 10.

With the finished vessel, I felt my anxieties yielding to a sense of confidence. I think I will do another—this time larger and out of mesquite!

MASHRABEYA—

No rain fell during the eight weeks we were in Cairo—none. Average rainfall in the area is less than 1 inch annually. In this climate, mashrabeya fits right in. William Lyster says in his article, "Places in Egypt— 1989," *mashrabeya* means, literally, "a drinking thing". This refers to the use of mashrabeya to enclose unglazed earthenware water bottles placed in windows to cool the air that ventilates houses in the hot desert climate.

As Lyster describes it, mashrabeya is "a series of balls connected to each other by cylindrical links, forming a gridlike pattern. The arrangement of balls and links can become incredibly complex by increasing the number of elements added to the basic grill. Particularly well-made mashrabeya can have as many as 2,000 pieces within a square meter of grillwork."

Mashrabeya was initially used primarily for window shutters or screens so that medieval ladies of well-to-do houses could view the activity of the street without having to wear veils. (It is forbidden in Islamic society for them to reveal their faces.) Balconies and doorways as well as windows throughout the older sections of Cairo still display this distinctly Egyptian craft. In addition to complex geometric designs, mashrabeya is also used for silhouettes of pictures or words.

As architectural elements, these intriguing panels are incorporated into the design of furniture and other objects. Cabinets were, and still are, decorated with hundreds of turnings, as are tables, chairs, and boxes. It seems the more complex the design, the greater the pride in display.

30 CARVED-THROUGH LIDDED VESSEL

Here is a challenge for your turning and carving skills that will produce a piece that will be prized for generations.

Construction

The project uses a four-piece construction technique that will develop the parts from which the vessel will be assembled. This method allows you to have access for carving the difficult-to-reach areas. This access is also a real benefit while doing the indexing and drawing.

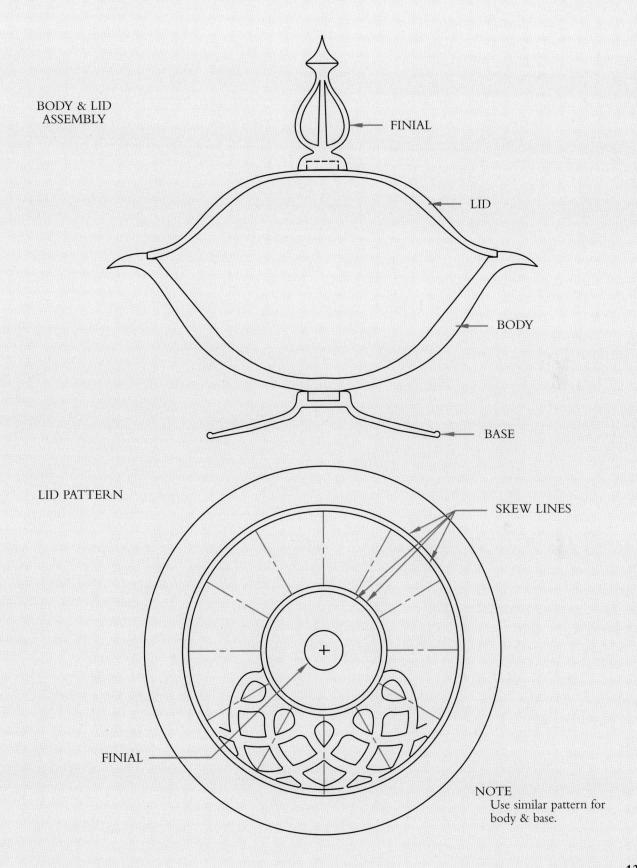

BODY & LID
ASSEMBLY

FINIAL

LID

BODY

BASE

LID PATTERN

SKEW LINES

FINIAL

NOTE
Use similar pattern for
body & base.

139

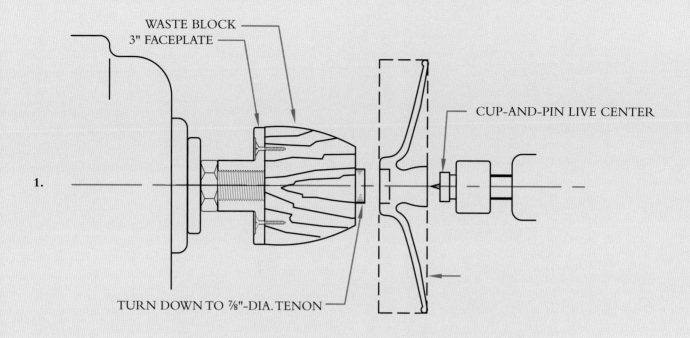

1.

WASTE BLOCK
3" FACEPLATE

CUP-AND-PIN LIVE CENTER

TURN DOWN TO ⅞"-DIA. TENON

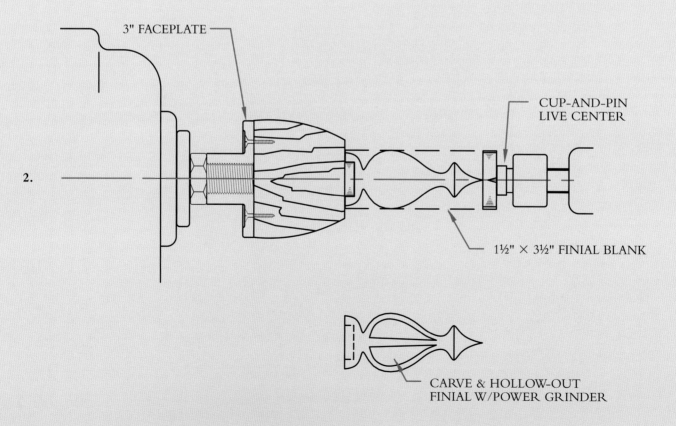

2.

3" FACEPLATE

CUP-AND-PIN
LIVE CENTER

1½" × 3½" FINIAL BLANK

CARVE & HOLLOW-OUT
FINIAL W/POWER GRINDER

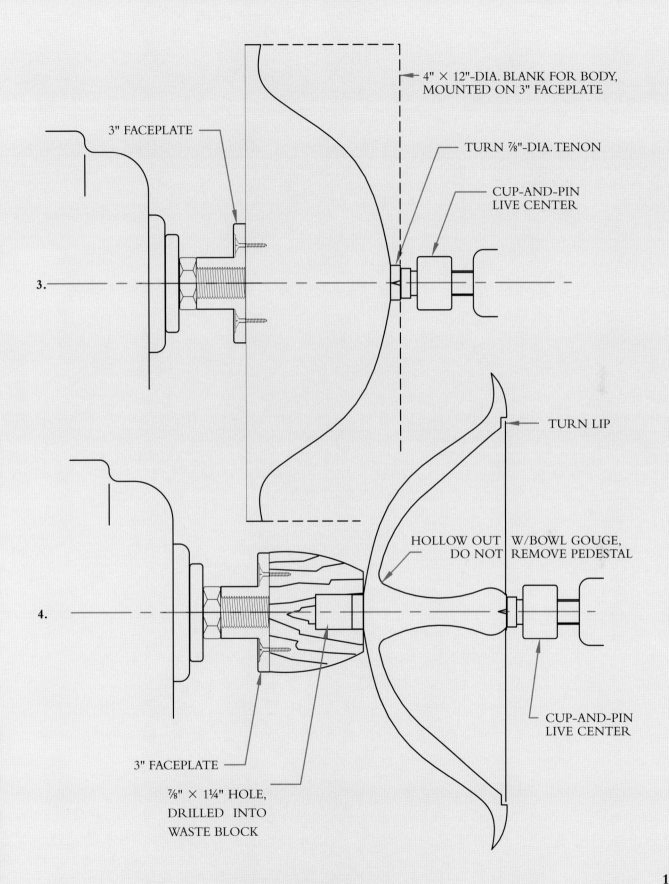

3.

4" × 12"-DIA. BLANK FOR BODY,
MOUNTED ON 3" FACEPLATE

3" FACEPLATE

TURN ⅞"-DIA. TENON

CUP-AND-PIN
LIVE CENTER

TURN LIP

4.

3" FACEPLATE

⅞" × 1¼" HOLE,
DRILLED INTO
WASTE BLOCK

HOLLOW OUT W/BOWL GOUGE,
DO NOT REMOVE PEDESTAL

CUP-AND-PIN
LIVE CENTER

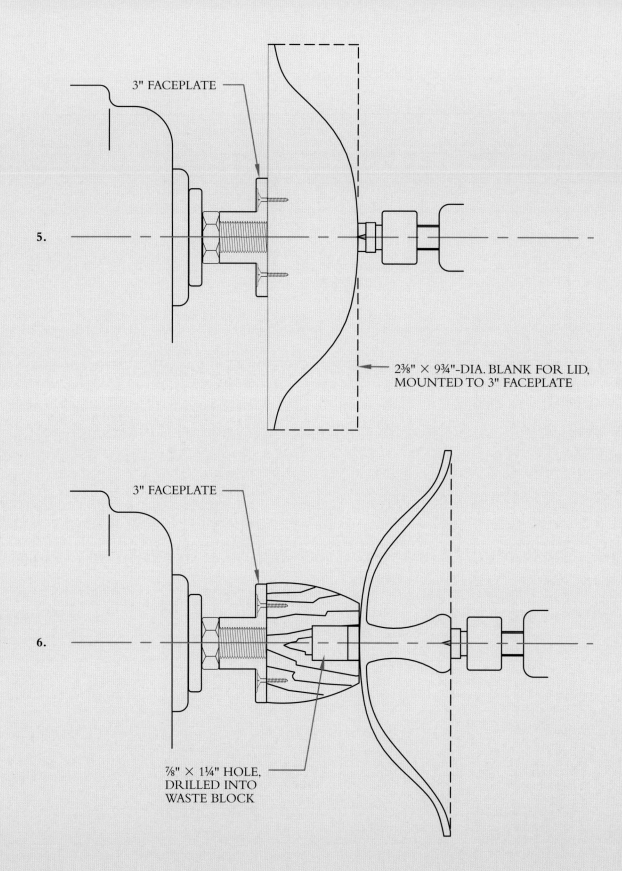

5.

3" FACEPLATE

2⅜" × 9¾"-DIA. BLANK FOR LID,
MOUNTED TO 3" FACEPLATE

6.

3" FACEPLATE

⅞" × 1¼" HOLE,
DRILLED INTO
WASTE BLOCK

Making the Base

- The base blank is band-sawed to 6½" in diameter by 1¼" thick. In the top of the blank, drill a ⅞" hole ¼" deep with a Forstner bit. A 3" faceplate-mounted waste block about 2" long is turned down at the front to 2" diameter.
- Then turn a tenon ⅞" diameter by ¼" long to act as a mandrel for the base turning (see drawings).
- Bring up the tailstock with a cup-and-pin live center to secure the blank against the waste-block mandrel. Use your favorite spindle gouge or bowl gouge. This configuration is just like turning a bowl.
- With figure-eight calipers, check wall thickness regularly. Other than the bead at the edge, which improves structural integrity, turn the wall to a consistent ⅛" thickness.

Do not remove the pedestal created by holding the piece in place until after the carving is finished. You may have to put it back in the lathe for drawing the concentric circles for the carving pattern. It can be removed last with a bench chisel and the small area hand sanded (see "Sanding Suggestions" and "Finishes" earlier, on pages 8, 9, and 10).

Put one coat of finish on the piece. This helps reduce transferring oils from your hands while carving. It also protects for covering with drafting tape.

There will be eight basic patterns, but each must have a centerline; thus index the base into 16 sections—360 degrees divided by 16 segments equals 22.5 degrees (see "Lathe Indexing" on pages 10 and 11). The process for laying out and carving the pattern on the tape is described in the sidebar.

Making the Body & Lid

- Mount the body of the project on a 3" faceplate after band-sawing out a 4" thick × 12" diameter blank.

Check grain direction in all pieces before drilling or turning to make sure you have the right side up. Laying all the pieces out after band-sawing and marking them before turning will help keep the grain direction correct.

- Turn a ⅞" tenon ¼" long that will serve two purposes. First, it will be the mounting joint to be placed in a ⅞"-diameter × 1¼"-deep drilled hole

CARVING THE PATTERNS—

- Establish the critical points of intersection of the pattern on the indexed piece.
- Shade the areas to be removed to make sure you do not take out the wrong piece.
- Drill a hole in each area to be removed with a hand drill. This will relieve the area and make it easier to remove the wood.

Use power to carve and sand as much as possible. A handheld power carver such as Optima II™ or Foredom™ will make the carving process more enjoyable—and a lot faster. A split mandrel for making a flap sander to be held in the rotary tool works really well.

in the same waste block to turn the inside, and second, it will be the mounting tenon when the base is glued to the body when the project is assembled.

- The outside of the body is turned first, then removed from the faceplate and reversed to turn the inside. Use the tailstock as when the base was turned.
- The lid is turned with the same procedure except that the blank is 2⅜" thick × 9¾" in diameter.

Indexing on the body and lid is in 6 pattern repetitions that will require 12 indexed sections—360 degrees divided by 12 sections equal 30 degrees. The process for laying out and carving the pattern on the tape is described in the sidebar.

Making the Finial

The finial blank is drilled before turning to fit the tenon on the top. Although it is optional depending on the taste of the turner, a carved finial on a carved turning adds that extra degree of workmanship and pride.

- The blank is 1½" diameter by 3½" long and turned as in the above procedure.

This project really is not as time-consuming as it looks at first. The disciplines practiced and perfected in this piece are great skills to have in your memory bank.

31 SPIRAL-GROOVED VESSEL

Tigerwood was chosen for this project—but this piece has nothing to do with golfing. This is just the name of a very lovely wood you can use for turning or carving. Tigerwood is the name used to describe a beautifully streaked black and brown cabinetmaker's wood, sometimes called itakawood—especially when it is from Guyana in South America—but typically it is African walnut.

This is one of those afternoon projects that will usually expand to take up your whole day. As they say, "Time flies when you are having fun!" This is a great way to enjoy turning. You will find that having a four-jaw chuck helps this project work smoothly.

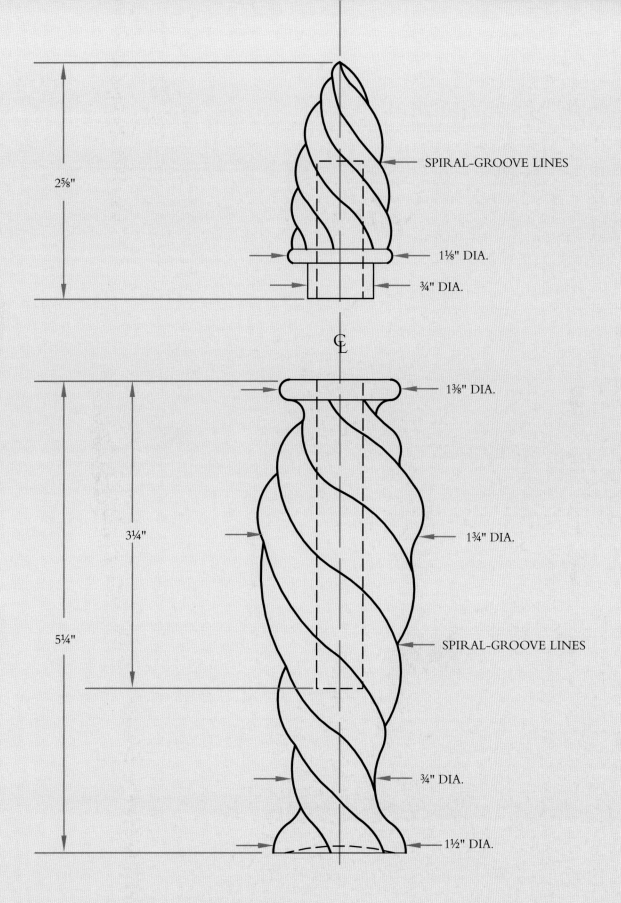

2⅝"

SPIRAL-GROOVE LINES

1⅛" DIA.

¾" DIA.

C̶L

1⅜" DIA.

3¼"

1¾" DIA.

SPIRAL-GROOVE LINES

5¼"

¾" DIA.

1½" DIA.

145

Selecting the Wood

Choose a really hard wood with nice graining to get the best results. You will need to start out with a 1¾" × 1¾" × 9½" blank.

❖ Saw off a 3½" piece for the top and a 6" piece for the body.

SPIRAL GROOVES—

When you are through turning and are ready to start sanding the spiral grooves, instead of indexing to work within specific disciplined areas, this time take a pencil and draw some random spiral lines from the base to below the flange on the body and from the flange on the lid up to the tip.

❖ Use a 1½"-to-2" sanding disk with a rubber back in the Jacobs chuck mounted in the headstock.
❖ Hold the turning at about 60 degrees to the disk. Start with 120-grit and sand each side of the groove.
❖ Lines are a little hard to follow at this stage, but the finer grits will work easier.
❖ After the lines are started, use 150-, 180-, 220-, 240-, 320-, and 400-grit paper.

Inspect closely the surface to see that you have not left scratches before you go to the next higher grit. A rubber cleaning block will add life to your sanding disk when used regularly.

❖ By the time you are using 220-grit, cover the entire surface to soften the spiral lines.

When you are using the coarser grits, you will think you have ruined the piece, but you will be glad if you continue.

❖ Mark the saw kerf of each side so that you can make sure that your connection later will make the grain match.

Turning the Body

Mount in the chuck the turning blank for the body that is 1¾" square × 6" long. This allows for some waste to be left in the chuck. The marked saw kerf will be toward the tailstock.

❖ Drill a ¾" hole with a Forstner bit 3¼" deep.

Bring up the tailstock with a small cone on the live center. Insert the cone in the drilled hole and exert a light pressure to secure the piece between the live center and the chuck (see the drawing).

❖ Turn the profile of the example or design your own. Sand and finish (see "Sanding Suggestions" and "Finishes" earlier, on pages 8, 9, and 10).
❖ Use a parting tool to part the piece from the chuck. Remember to always make the base slightly concave so that it will set steadily on the table.
❖ Use a 2" sanding disk mounted in a Jacobs chuck in the headstock to sand the base.

Turning the Top

❖ Use the four-jaw chuck for making the top out of the 3½"-long blank. The marked saw kerf will again be toward the tailstock.
❖ Drill as above, a ½" hole 1" deep.

Again bring up the live center with a small cone to insert in the drill hole.

❖ Turn a ¾"-diameter tenon on the end of the piece to fit in the drilled hole of the body. Turn the shape in the drawing but leave a ¼" connection to the chuck.
❖ Turn off the lathe and saw the top from the chuck at the small ¼" connection.

Making the Grooves

Now that you are done turning it is time to have some fun making the spiral grooves, as detailed in the sidebar.

32

FLORAL CARVED VESSEL

This project presents a different type of turning and wall penetration in that the turned surfaces to be carved are of varying diameters. Also, the patterns are floral in design and the holes are smaller.

The indexing system is the same as that used for other carved and turned vessels, but in this project the entire pattern is repeated eight times. Although they will appear as running patterns when finished, each section is separate.

In planning and preparing this project, it is recommended that all the blanks be measured and cut out on a band saw before going to the lathe. This will let you check grain direction and mark all the pieces as to top or bottom. This eliminates the possibility of turning a piece with the wrong side up and having a mismatch on the grain. Good planning pays well.

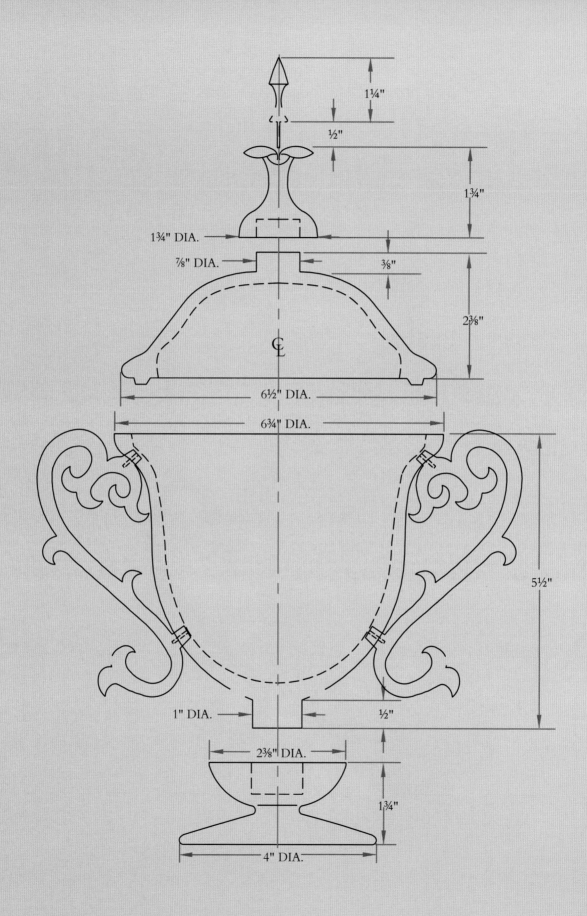

1¼"

½"

1¾"

1¾" DIA.

⅞" DIA.

⅜"

2⅜"

ℂℒ

6½" DIA.

6¾" DIA.

5½"

1" DIA.

½"

2⅜" DIA.

1¾"

4" DIA.

HANDLE PATTERN

2"

4"

BRASS-PIN
INSERT →

BRASS-PIN
INSERT →

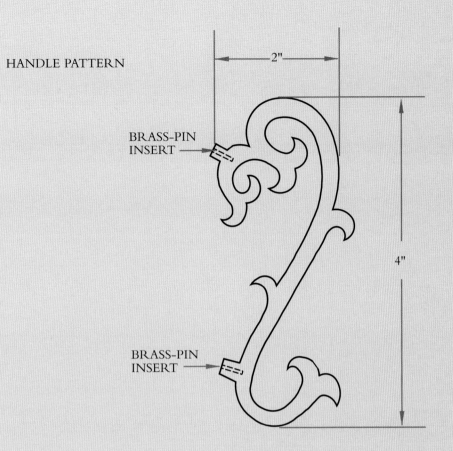

LID PATTERN

SKEW LINES

BODY PATTERN

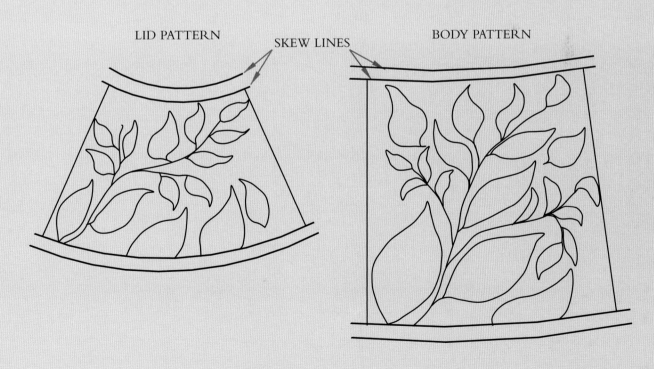

Turning the Base & Body

The base is turned using a 3" faceplate with an attached waste block. Use C/A glue to attach a 1½" × 4"-diameter blank that has been band-sawed round.

❖ Using the tailstock with a Jacobs chuck, drill a 1"-diameter hole ½" in the blank. Remove the drill chuck from the tailstock and bring up a cup-and-pin live center to secure the turning. (See drawing.)
❖ Use your favorite spindle gouge and shape the base.
❖ Use the parting tool to part away only enough of the underside of the base to make it concave. Remove the base from the waste block by parting off the waste-block side of the glue joint.

Reverse the base and set up in a four-jaw chuck expanding the pin jaws into the drilled hole. Turn, detail, sand and finish the piece. (See "Sanding Suggestions" and "Finishes" earlier, on pages 8, 9, and 10.)

❖ The body is turned first by fastening what will be the top of the opening to a 3" faceplate and turning the exterior.
❖ Turn a 1" tenon on the bottom to fit into the base. Sand and finish the outside of the body and remove it from the faceplate.

Secure the body tenon in a four-jaw chuck, paying careful attention to center and balance. Bring up the tailstock to secure the piece between centers. Measure and turn the groove into which the lid will fit.

Leave the tailstock in place and work around it as long as you can (see the sidebar, "Wall Thickness"). This procedure is well worth the effort because it adds stability and safety in keeping down chuck and glue failures.

Carving the Floral Pattern

❖ Make two skew lines on each side of the area to be carved to "frame" the carvings.
❖ Cover the carving area with drafting tape so that you can draw directly on the surface.

Index into eight segments—360 degrees divided by 8 equals 45 degrees. Make a pattern blank of one segment on paper and draw the pattern to be carved on the blank. Use carbon paper to transfer the pattern to the tape on each section.

This same procedure is used on both body and lid. The lid is turned using the same procedure as the body, except the tenon will be smaller (see drawings).

Carving away the areas indicated by the pattern is not that difficult if you have a reversible, high-speed mini-grinder. Drill a hole in the center of each area to gain entry of the burr. A split mandrel in the grinder turned at slow speed makes an excellent flap sander.

Making the Finial & Handles

Turn the finial base in a four-jaw chuck. Drill the hole that will fit over the tenon on the lid with a Jacobs chuck in the tailstock. The flower-shaped carving is indexed at 6 segments—360 degrees divided by 6 equals 60 degrees. Drill a ⅛" hole ½" deep in the center of the flower for the finial insert.

Turn the finial insert either between centers or with a Jacobs chuck. After carving the flower, insert it into the drilled hole.

To make the handles see the sidebar "Making the Handles" on page 131. Check tenon angles to make sure they fit. The same mini-grinders can eliminate a lot but not all of the hand work on the handles. Some hand sanding with finer grits will be necessary.

WALL THICKNESS—

As a discipline, you should always maintain the desired thickness from the outer edge toward the bottom as you progress. Most woods will have some distortion when stress-relieved by turning. In making your finished cuts as you gain depth, you will not have to come back to an area that has already distorted. Sanding the area after the vessel is complete is not a problem. Catches generally occur when you go back to the area that has stress-relieved while you were turning and is now out of round. On thin vessels, one catch and usually you start over. The problem is resolved by finishing your cuts as you go. Consistent wall thickness is a necessity in the carved area.

150

33 IZZY A. TURNER

While making a tradition-al music box as a gift, I noticed that the winding key offered a surprising amount of torque when I tried to hold it to stop the music. It occurred to me that it might be possible to use this power in some way to animate additional designs that could be incorporated into a turned music box. A number of the projects in this book use this concept (see, for example, the side-bar "How it Rotates," on page 57).

When you wind up Izzy's nose, his eyes roll around slowly, the propeller rotates on the top of the cap, and his nose turns while he plays your choice of music.

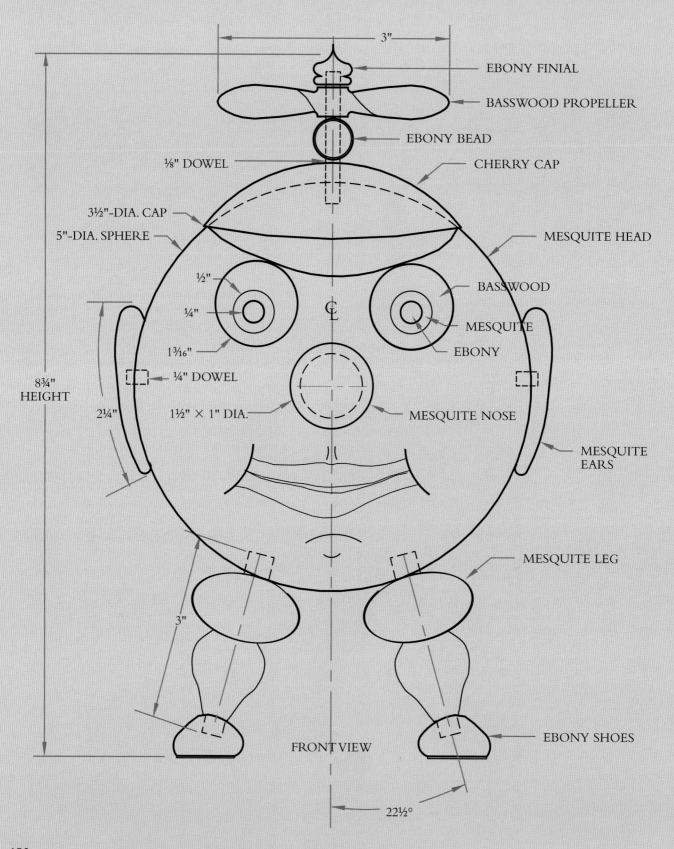

EBONY FINIAL

BASSWOOD PROPELLER

EBONY BEAD

⅛" DOWEL

CHERRY CAP

3½"-DIA. CAP

MESQUITE HEAD

5"-DIA. SPHERE

½"

¼"

BASSWOOD

MESQUITE

1³⁄₁₆"

EBONY

¼" DOWEL

8¾"
HEIGHT

2¼"

1½" × 1" DIA.

MESQUITE NOSE

MESQUITE
EARS

MESQUITE LEG

3"

EBONY SHOES

FRONT VIEW

22½°

152

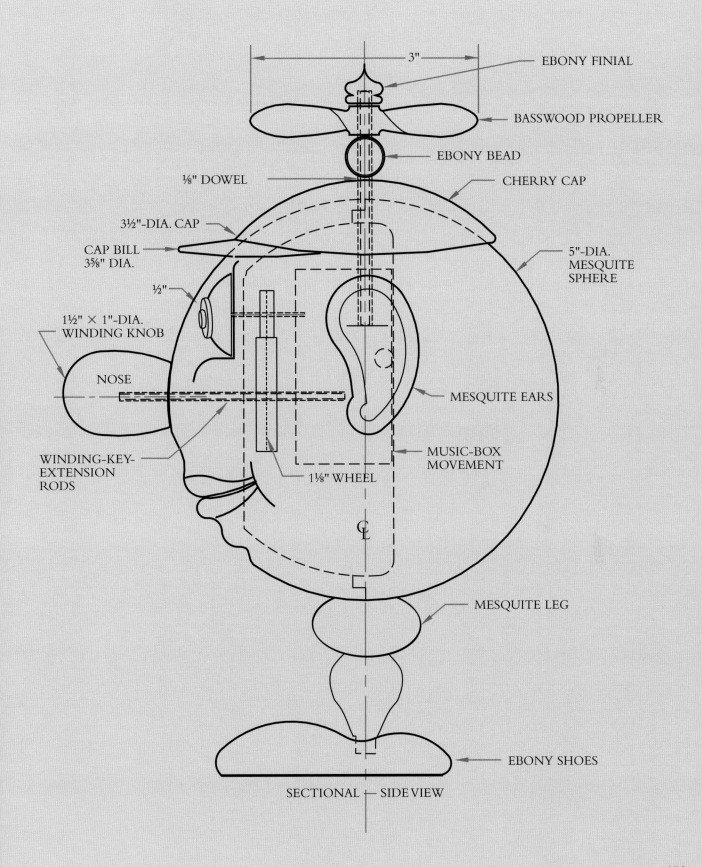

3"

EBONY FINIAL

BASSWOOD PROPELLER

EBONY BEAD

⅛" DOWEL

CHERRY CAP

3½"-DIA. CAP

CAP BILL
3⅝" DIA.

5"-DIA.
MESQUITE
SPHERE

½"

1½" × 1"-DIA.
WINDING KNOB

NOSE

MESQUITE EARS

WINDING-KEY-
EXTENSION
RODS

MUSIC-BOX
MOVEMENT

1⅛" WHEEL

C L

MESQUITE LEG

EBONY SHOES

SECTIONAL — SIDE VIEW

SPHERE-TURNING SEQUENCE

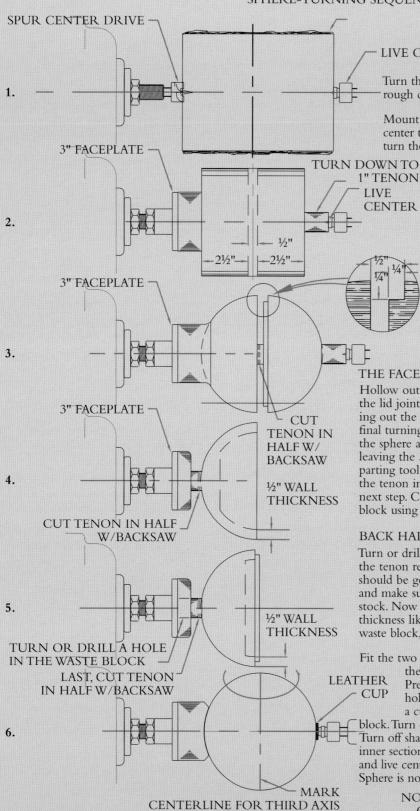

SPUR CENTER DRIVE

LIVE CENTER

1.

Turn the blank between spur center and live center to a rough dimension of 5¼" × 10".

3" FACEPLATE

TURN DOWN TO 1" TENON

LIVE CENTER

2.

½"

2½" 2½"

Mount to rough cylinder to a 3"-diameter faceplate. Re-center tailstock and retrue the rough blank. Using calipers, turn the cylinder to 5" finished diameter. Mark parallel pencil lines ½" apart indicating where the sphere will be separated. Mark another line 2½" out from the first lines. With spindle gouge remove the waste stock. Turn headstock end to a 3" tenon. Turn tailstock end to a 1" tenon.

3" FACEPLATE

½" ¼"

¼" ¼"

3.

Between the two center lines is where the sphere will be separated. Begin by taking a ⅛" parting tool, cut in about 2" deep inside the left line. With the same tool on the right side, cut only about ¼" down and ¼" wide, forming the lid joint. With a spindle gouge, rough-form both halves of the sphere into an oval shape, working out 2½" from the ½" gap to the outside tenons. Using a backsaw, separate the two halves.

3" FACEPLATE

CUT TENON IN HALF W/ BACKSAW

½" WALL THICKNESS

4.

THE FACE HALF OF THE HEAD

Hollow out the half still attached to the faceplate. Complete the lid joint to fit the two pieces back together. When hollowing out the bowl, leave the wall about ½" thick to allow for final turning to a true sphere. With a spindle gouge, round out the sphere and turn down the waste block behind the sphere, leaving the 3"-diameter waste block about 2" long. With a parting tool cut the face of the waste block smooth down to the tenon in preparation for drilling the tenon hole in the next step. Cut off the first half of the sphere from the waste block using a backsaw.

CUT TENON IN HALF W/BACKSAW

3" FACEPLATE

½" WALL THICKNESS

5.

TURN OR DRILL A HOLE IN THE WASTE BLOCK

LAST, CUT TENON IN HALF W/BACKSAW

BACK HALF OF THE HEAD

Turn or drill a hole in the waste block the same diameter as the tenon remaining on the other half of the sphere. This fit should be good and tight. Glue the tenon in the faceplate hole and make sure that it turns true before brining up the tailstock. Now hollow out the second half, keeping the ½" wall thickness like the first half. Cut off the second half from the waste block, allowing for the final rounding of the sphere.

LEATHER CUP

6.

MARK CENTERLINE FOR THIRD AXIS

Fit the two halves together and finish-turn the sphere using the three-axis system for final turning and sanding. Prepare a waste block attached to a 3" faceplate and hollow to fit the sphere diameter. Use a leather pad on a cup center to hold the sphere against the waste block. Turn off the tenon stubs until round. Mark the 2nd axis. Turn off shadow image only. Remark the 2nd axis. Rotate the inner section of the 1st and 2nd axes to between waste block and live center. Turn off only shadow image. Mark 3rd axis. Sphere is now round. Sand on same axis rotation in each grit.

NOTE
Change axes to original (three times) while turning each grit of sandpaper.

Preparing the Pieces

To get the project underway, band-saw out a blank 5¼" diameter by 10" long. If you are unable to do this in your band saw, then turn the blank between centers to this size and square the ends for faceplate mounting.

❖ Mount the turned or sawed blank on a 3" faceplate. Bring up the tailstock for safety, and true up the piece again.

❖ Use calipers to measure the diameter of the turned cylinder, which for this project should be about 5".

❖ Make two pencil lines in the center of the blank about ½" apart. This is where the sphere will be separated and will, also, form the lip so that the two halves can be fitted back together again.

One half of the sphere will fit into the other the same as on a lidded box. The ½" gap will maximize grain match and minimize wood waste (see drawing).

❖ On one side of the gap, make a ⅛" parting-tool cut approximately 2" deep.

❖ On the other side, with the same tool, cut about ¼" deep and ¼" wide. This forms the lip or tenon for the connection later.

Measure from the edge of the gap each direction one-half of the previously established diameter and make a line. This will form one-half of the sphere.

❖ Make about a 2"-deep cut with a parting tool.

❖ With a spindle gouge, rough-form the halves of the sphere to an oval shape from the gap to the tenon. Do not reduce the diameter of the gap.

❖ With a backsaw, separate the two halves.

Hollowing Out

You can now hollow the half still attached to the faceplate and make the lid joint to fit the two pieces back together.

❖ Use figure-eight calipers to check wall thickness. Leave the walls about ½" thick to allow for wood loss when it is turned later into a true sphere. The lid joint is thick enough to make this allowance.

Be careful when making the jointed pieces; the fit needs to be snug to hold the finished piece together. No sanding is necessary inside the sphere (see "Sanding Suggestions" and "Finishes," on pages 8, 9, and 10).

SPHERE & MUSIC BOX—

Spheres are always both challenging and rewarding. This project incorporates a number of different turning techniques, carving disciplines, and just plain fun. Also refer to Project Number. 15 for turning spheres (see pages 75–76, as well as page 154).

The music box is placed inside the hollowed sphere and the winding-key shaft has been extended to a knob-shaped nose (see "Adding a Music Box," on page 51; I used the Sankyo 18-note, see page 156). The drum inside this specific music box has a hollow shaft with a ⅛" inside diameter. By positioning the music box so that the music drum is vertical, I could insert a ⅛" dowel through the top of the sphere to turn a small propeller on top of Izzy's cap.

I thought it would be unique if I could get the eyes to move or turn, along with the nose and the propeller on the cap. Making this idea work cost me a substantial amount of sleep, and a day on the lathe. Stubbornness finally prevailed and the eyes rolled steadily. I explain how this is accomplished in "The Rolling Eyes," on page 157.

❖ With a backsaw, cut off the first half from the waste block. Remember that the sphere oval continues into the tenon, so do not cut it too close or you will create a flat spot on the sphere.

❖ Turn or drill a hole in the waste block the same size as the tenon left on the other half that was next to the live center.

❖ Glue the half in place, making sure that it turns true before bringing up the tailstock.

You can now hollow out the second half making sure you have the same wall thickness as the first half.

❖ Cut off the second half from the waste block. Remember that the arc of the sphere continues into the tenon, as stated above.

Fitting the Halves Together

Fit the two halves together and turn into a sphere using the same three-axis system as described earlier in this book. Sanding the sphere is done on the same three axes as turning or you may sand it out of round.

❖ Apply a coat of finish to the surface to prevent staining the raw wood with finger prints and other unwanted mishaps.

Select one of the halves that will be the face of the figure. Drill a ³⁄₁₆" hole in the center of the half sphere by laying the joint side flat on the drill-press table. This will be for the winding key that holds the nose. Check grain

THE MOVEMENT—

The Sankyo 18-note music movement has a ⅛" hole in the drum shaft that has the pegs. This hole will be utilized to insert a ⅛" dowel that will go up through the cap and turn the propeller. If you want to leave the dustcover on the mechanism, you must drill a hole in the clear plastic cover. To do so, remove the cover to keep from leaving drill shavings inside the cover that could damage the mechanism. This adaptation acts as a right-angle gear box to power the propeller on top of the cap. The ⅛" dowel can easily be removed and reinserted for assembly. You will need to make some adjustments as you complete the project and this feature is very useful.

When ordering your music box (see page 51), be sure to order four key extensions. They are not listed in the current catalog so you must ask for them. They come in different lengths, and if you get three ¾" long and one ¼" long, you will be able to find a combination that works. The depth of the hole in the nose piece will act as a point of adjustments to establish the correct length of the winding shaft.

alignment to choose a direction that will become the top of the figure when finished. Place a piece of drafting tape from the top to the bottom of the hemisphere. Mark a centerline from the drilled ³⁄₁₆" hole to the top center.

Making the Face

The eyes will be placed 1" above the nose and 1" to each side of this centerline.

❖ Use a 1" Forstner bit and drill a slight depression for each eye. The side toward the centerline will be about ³⁄₁₆" deep and the outside will be only to the surface because of the placement of the eye 1" off center.

❖ The mouth is centered and drawn on drafting tape.

Since the face of the figure is oval, the mouth should be full and the cheeks round. Undercut the bottom lip to create the chin.

❖ To carve the mouth area, I used a high-speed hand-held grinder with flame-shaped burr.

❖ Using the centerpoint mark left by the Forstner bit in the eye socket, drill a ⅛" hole at an angle toward the center of the sphere. This will be for the ⅛" brass shaft that will make the eyes rotate.

Making the Eyes

❖ To make the whites of the eyes, use a light-colored wood such as hackberry, holly, or basswood. Turn a disk ¼" thick by 1³⁄₁₆" diameter.

❖ To make the pupil of the eye, use a scrap of wood from the sphere so that a part of the wood in the eye matches the figure, and turn two ½" disks ¼" thick.

❖ The center of the pupil is made of dark hardwood, such as ebony or walnut. This is turned as a spindle, ¼" diameter × about ¾" long, which allows for wood loss in the saw kerf. Cut off two ¼"-long pieces.

❖ Drill holes in the disk of the proper size, insert, and glue up the different-colored woods. This will produce a realistic eye with three colors of wood.

❖ To shape the eye disk, use a 1" dowel held in a chuck or waste block and flatten the front with a parting tool. Use double-stick tape to mount the eye disk ¼" off-center. Hold the disk in place with a cup-type live center covered with a leather pad until it is turned to 1" round.

When the disk is round, you can then release the live center and form the eye disk into an oval shape. With the darker-wood part of the eye off-center, it will be noticeable when the eye turns as the music plays. Drill a ⅛" hole ⅛" deep in the back of the finished eye disk. This will be used to glue the eye disk to the brass shaft (see the sidebar "The Rolling Eyes" for completing the eye mechanism).

Turning the Nose

The nose is turned using a drill chuck mounted in the headstock.

❖ Drill a ³⁄₁₆" hole ¾" deep in a 1"-diameter × 1½" long blank. The grain direction of the nose should be the same as the area of the sphere to which it will be mounted.

❖ Place a short piece of ³⁄₁₆" dowel in the drill chuck. The blank is mounted on the dowel and held in place with a cup-type live center covered with a leather pad. To sand the nose, the tailstock can be removed to allow access to the front of the piece.

Turning the Cap & Finial

The cap on the figure's head is turned out of a contrasting wood color.

❖ Mount a waste block on a 3" faceplate or four-jaw chuck. Turn the end of the waste block down to 1½" diameter and drill a ⅛" hole in the center.

❖ Insert and glue in place another short length of ⅛" brass rod, the same as used for the eyes.

The cap blank is 6" diameter by 1" thick with a ⅛" hole through the center. Mount on the waste block with double-stick tape. Use the tailstock with a large-point live center to hold the blank in place.

❖ Turn the outside shape of the cap.

❖ Make two skew lines at 3½" and 3⅝" diameter.

These will serve as a guide to band-saw out the shape of the cap when the piece is finished.

Remove the cap from the waste block and reverse the piece. Replace the double-stick tape and turn the inside as you did the outside.

❖ Use figure-eight calipers to achieve a consistent ⅛" thickness. A paper template will assist the effort to make the inside of the cap fit the top of the sphere.

THE ROLLING EYES—

Part of the mechanism needed to make the eyes roll has already been prepared as you made the face and constructed the eyes. Review those sections to make sure you are ready to complete the eye mechanism. To proceed, you will need a 1"-diameter × ½"-thick wheel to attach to the eye shaft on the inside of the sphere.

❖ To turn this, drill a ⅛" hole in two ½"-hick × 1¼"-diameter blanks.

❖ Place a drill chuck in the headstock and insert a short piece of ⅛" brass rod. The blanks are placed on the brass rod and held in place with a large-point live center.

❖ Turn round like a car tire and do not sand. They will need some friction to turn the eye shaft.

I used a coat of beeswax applied to the wheels while turning. It worked very well.

To make the eyes turn, I used a wheel made from a gum-rubber sandpaper-cleaner block.

❖ This was band-sawed off of the block ½" thick and drilled with a ³⁄₁₆" hole in the center.

❖ The same setup was used that turned the nose to turn it to about 1⅛" diameter.

You may have to adjust this diameter slightly to compensate for the wheels on the inside of the sphere that connects to the eyes. This gum-rubber wheel will mount on the inside of the sphere on the same shaft that holds the nose in place and screws into the music mechanism. The eye wheels should touch the rubber wheel.

Before sawing out the shape of the cap, choose a grain direction for the bill or front of the cap that looks best.

The same chuck system is used to turn the spacer and the finial that go on the propeller shaft.

Carving the Ears

The ears are carved from a scrap of the same wood as the sphere and held in place with ¼" dowels. The length of the ear should be about one-third the diameter of the sphere. When you are positioning the ear on the turning, the top of the ear should be level with the center of the eye. Grain direction should be matched to the area of the sphere to which it will be attached. A ¼" tenon turned from the same wood will serve as the method of attachment.

SPLIT-TURNING—

The shoes, or feet, are another interesting exercise in woodturning. This time, you will use a split-turning procedure to assure that both shoes are symmetrical.

❖ Rough turn a blank 1⅛" diameter × 3½" long out of the same dark wood used for the cap.
❖ Use a bandsaw to saw it into halves split down the grain.
❖ Sand off the saw marks on a flat-belt sander, taking care to remove no more wood than is necessary.

Use double-stick tape to put the two halves back together.

❖ To turn the final shape, turn a ¼"-deep depression in a waste block to fit the 1⅛"-diameter blank.

A cup-type live center will provide friction and support to hold the blank in place.

❖ Turn the shape with a spindle gouge and sand the ends.
❖ Drill the holes for the leg tenons about 1" from the heel so that the turning will not fall over on its backside.

Turning the Legs

The chubby legs are turned between centers as spindles. The blank should be 1½" diameter × 3" long. Turn the legs 2" long with 5/16" diameter × ⅜"long tenons. (See drawing.)

For the shoes or feet, see the sidebar "Split-Turning."

The Propeller

❖ To drill the hole in the top of the sphere for the propeller shaft, put the two sphere halves together and mark the center of the joint and the center of the spheres directly above the hole drilled for the nose.
❖ Drill the hole directly through the joint.

Holding the sphere steady for drilling is easy if you lay a roll of masking or duct tape on the drill-press table and set the sphere on the tape roll.

Adding the Music Mechanism

No support bracket is necessary to hold the music mechanism in place. The ⅛" dowel that fits on the propeller and down through the cap will fit directly into the hollow drum shaft. From the other direction, the winding shaft that goes from the mechanism to the nose screws onto the music box.

❖ Adjust the position of the mechanism by varying the length of the nose or winding shaft.

This was the reason for drilling the extra depth in the nose for the winding shaft. Once the position is established, a small drop of C/A glue will secure the shaft to the nose.

Final Adjustments

Check for binding of the shafts as you do the final assembly. It takes very little friction to stall the tiny motor in the music box.

If the music plays, the eyes roll, the nose turns, and the propeller rotates, you may have just created a new member of the family—but Izzy A. Turner?

Index

Adding a music box mechanism, 51, 112, 158
Another Blooming Mesquite, 37–41

Balancing, a sphere, 108
Ballet, Music Box, 52–54
Base
  concave, 123
  strengthening, 36
  turning. See specific projects
Bird-Watcher's Carousel Music Box, 55–58
Box
  designing your own, 68
  Lidded, with Push-Button Music, 66–67
  music. See Music box
  Scallop Shell Lidded, 109–112
Buffing process, 10
By The Numbers, 23–27

Candle Holder With Carved Through Chimney, 121–123
Canopy
  carving, 58
  turning, 58, 87
Carved-Edge Platter, 118–120
Carved-Through Lidded Vessel, 138–143
Carving
  canopy, 58
  figures, 54, 57–58
  floral pattern, 150
  grooves, 145
  mesquite, 41
  patterns, 143
  platter edge, 120
  shell pattern, 36, 112
  spiral pattern, 123, 145
Centerline, establishing, 64–65
Chatter work, 117

Decanter, Viny Mesquite, 18–22

Figures, carved, 54, 57–58
Finials
  designing, 27
  turning. See specific projects
Finishes, 9–10. See also specific projects
Flask
  Hollow, 124–127
  Mesquite Twister, 28–32
  By The Numbers, 23–27
  Shell-Carved Vertical Hollow, 28–36
  Viny Mesquite Decanter, 18–22
Floral Carved Vessel, 146–150
Flowers, mesquite, 37–41
Flying Birds Carousel Music Box, 80–83
Flying Saucer Music Box, 59–65
Foot, adding/turning, 48

Golden rectangle proportion, 26

Handled Urn, 128–131
Handles
  designing, 27
  making, 131, 150
Hollow Flask, 124–127
Hollowing out, 111, 155
Horse Carousel Music Box, 77–79

Image transfer, 58
Indexing
  cylinder, 123
  lathe, 10–11
  vessel design, 136
Inlayed patterns, 68, 111
"Izzy A. Turner," 151–158

Jaw clutch, winding, 83

Lathe
  indexing, 10–11
  safety guidelines, 7–8
  speed control, 63, 120

"Let-The-Good-Times-Roll" Music Box, 72–76
Lidded Box with Push-Button Music, 66–67
Lid turning. See specific projects

Mandrel, 99
Marquetry, 68, 111
Mashrabeya Vessel, 132–137
Measurement
  golden rectangle proportion, 26
  "one-third-two-thirds" rule, 26
Mesquite
  bending, 32
  carving, 41
  flowers, 37–41
  lumber, 16, 17
  shaping, 41
  Twister, 28–32
  twisting & bending, 41
  Vessel, 12–17
  Viny Decanter, 18–22
Music box
  Ballet, 52–54
  Bird-Watcher's Carousel, 55–58
  Flying Birds Carousel, 80–83
  Flying Saucer, 59–65
  Horse Carousel, 77–79
  "Izzy A. Turner," 151–158
  "Let-The-Good-Times-Roll," 72–76
  Lidded, with Push-Button Music, 66–67
  mechanism, adding, 51, 112, 158
  Sankyo 18 note movement, 156
  Scrap Wood, 49–51
  springs for, 57
  Traditional Turned, 69–71

Pincushion, 87
Pincushion holder, 99–100
Pinwheel Swirl Vessel, 101–104
Platter, Carved-Edge, 118–120

Ring, turning, 45
Rings of Saturn, 105–108
Rotating assembly, making, 57, 79

Safety, 7–8, 22, 63
Sanding, 8–9
Scales of Justice, 113–117
Scallop Shell Lidded Box, 109–112
Scrap Wood Music Box, 49–51
Sewing Tidy with Thimble, 89–92
Shell-Carved Vertical Hollow Flask, 28–36
Skills, sharing, 136
Sphere
    balancing, 108
    turning, 75–76, 154–155
Spiral-Grooved Vessel, 144–145

Split-turning, 158
Spools, wooden, 88, 100
Spool Tidy, 93–100
Surface decorations, 48, 104. *See also* Carving

Template, making, 104
Thimble, Sewing Tidy with, 89–92
Thread caddy, 99–100
Thread Dispenser with Hidden Drawer, 84–88
Traditional Turned Music Box, 69–71
Turned Wine-Bottle Stand, 42–45
Twig Pot Fun, 46–47

Urn, Handled, 128–131

Vase, Twig Pot Fun, 46–47
Vessel
    Carved-Through Lidded, 138–143
    Floral Carved, 146–150
    Handled Urn, 128–131
    Hollow Flask, 124–127
    Mashrabeya, 132–137
    Mesquite, 12–17
    Pinwheel Swirl, 101–104
    Spiral-Grooved, 144–145
Viny Mesquite Decanter, 18–22

Wall thickness, 150
Wet-and-wipe finishing method, 10
Wheels, turning, 65
Wine-Bottle Stand, Turned, 42–45

Metric Equivalents *(to nearest 1 mm, 0.1 cm)*

inches	mm	cm	inches	mm	cm	inches	mm	cm
⅛	3	0.3	2½	64	6.4	13	330	33.0
¼	6	0.6	3	76	7.6	14	356	35.6
⅜	10	1.0	3½	89	8.9	15	381	38.1
½	13	1.3	4	102	10.2	16	406	40.6
⅝	16	1.6	5	127	12.7	17	432	43.2
¾	19	1.9	6	152	15.2	18	457	45.7
⅞	22	2.2	7	178	17.8	19	483	48.3
1	25	2.5	8	203	20.3	20	508	50.8
1¼	32	3.2	9	229	22.9	21	533	53.3
1½	38	3.8	10	254	25.4	22	559	55.9
1¾	44	4.4	11	279	27.9	23	584	58.4
2	51	5.1	12	305	30.5	24	610	61.0

Conversion Factors

1 mm	=	0.03937 inch	1 inch	=	25.400 mm	mm	=	millimeter
1 m	=	3.28083 feet	1 foot	=	304.801 mm	cm	=	centimeter
						m	=	meter